Delusions play a fundamental role in the history of psychology, philosophy and culture, dividing not only the mad from the sane but reason from unreason. Yet the very nature and extent of delusions are poorly understood. What are delusions? How do they differ from everyday errors or mistaken beliefs? Are they scientific categories?

In this superb, panoramic investigation of delusion Jennifer Radden explores these questions and more, unravelling a fascinating story that ranges from Descartes's demon to famous first-hand accounts of delusion, such as Daniel Schreber's *Memoirs of My Nervous Illness*.

Radden places delusion in both a clinical and cultural context and explores a fascinating range of themes: delusions as both individually and collectively held, including the phenomenon of *folies á deux*; spiritual and religious delusions, in particular what distinguishes normal religious belief from delusions with religious themes; how we assess those suffering from delusion from a moral standpoint; and how we are to interpret violent actions when they are the result of delusional thinking. As well as more common delusions, such as those of grandeur, she also discusses some of the most interesting and perplexing forms of clinical delusion, such as Cotard and Capgras.

Jennifer Radden is Professor of Philosophy and a former Chair of Philosophy at the University of Massachusetts, Boston, USA. She is well known for her work within philosophy of psychology and psychiatry. Her recent books include *Moody Minds Distempered: Essays in Melancholy and Depression* (2009) and, with John Sadler, *The Virtuous Psychiatrist: Character Ethics in Psychiatric Practice* (2010).

Thinking in Action

Series editors: Simon Critchley, The New School University, New York, and Richard Kearney, Boston College, USA, and University College Dublin

Thinking in Action is a major new series that takes philosophy to its public. Each book in the series is written by a major international philosopher or thinker, engages with an important contemporary topic, and is clearly and accessibly written. The series informs and sharpens debate on issues as wide ranging as the Internet, religion, the problem of immigration and refugees, criticism, architecture, and the way we think about science. Punchy, short and stimulating, **Thinking in Action** is an indispensable starting point for anyone who wants to think seriously about major issues confronting us today.

Praise for the series

". . . allows a space for distinguished thinkers to write about their passions."
The Philosophers' Magazine

". . . deserve high praise."
Boyd Tonkin, *The Independent (UK)*

"This is clearly an important series. I look forward to receiving future volumes."
Frank Kermode, author of *Shakespeare's Language*

"both rigorous and accessible"
Humanist News

"the series looks superb"
Quentin Skinner

". . . an excellent and beautiful series."
Ben Rogers, author of *A.J. Ayer: A Life*

"Routledge's Thinking in Action series is the theory junkie's answer to the eminently pocketable Penguin 60s series."
Mute Magazine (UK)

"Routledge's new series, *Thinking in Action*, brings philosophers to our aid . . ."
The Evening Standard (UK)

". . . a welcome series by Routledge"
Bulletin of Science, Technology and Society (Can)

"Routledge's innovative new 'Thinking in Action' series takes the concept of philosophy a step further"
The Bookwatch

JENNIFER RADDEN

On
Delusion

Routledge
Taylor & Francis Group

LONDON AND NEW YORK

This edition published 2011
by Routledge
2 Park Square, Milton Park, Abingdon, Oxon OX14 4RN

Simultaneously published in the USA and Canada
by Routledge
270 Madison Avenue, New York, NY 10016

Routledge is an imprint of the Taylor & Francis Group, an informa business

Typeset in Joanna and Din by
RefineCatch Ltd, Bungay, Suffolk
Printed and bound in Great Britain by
the MPG Books Group Ltd

British Library Cataloguing in Publication Data
A catalogue record for this book is available from the British Library

Library of Congress Cataloging-in-Publication Data
Radden, Jennifer.
  On delusion / Jennifer Radden.
    p. cm.—(Thinking in action)
  Includes bibliographical references and index.
  1. Delusions.   I. Title.
  RC553.D35.R33 2010
  616.89—dc22   2010004302

ISBN10: 0-415-77447-0 (hbk)
ISBN10: 0-415-77448-9 (pbk)
ISBN10: 0-203-84651-6 (ebk)

ISBN13: 978-0-415-77447-5 (hbk)
ISBN13: 978-0-415-77448-2 (pbk)
ISBN13: 978-0-203-84651-3 (ebk)

This book is dedicated to Frank Keefe.

Contents

Acknowledgements

My interest in clinical delusions has been nourished over the years by clinical tales and clinical wisdom from those working with delusional patients, by memoirs and other first-person accounts of disorder, and by students participating in a course on delusion and epistemology during the fall semester of 2008.

I must also acknowledge the support and enthusiasm I received from Tony Bruce as this project took shape, and the invaluable reviews provided by anonymous readers of the book's prospectus. My research assistant Dylan Rossi gave trusted and efficient aid for which I am thankful. My special thanks go to Fayez El Gabalawi, Amélie Rorty, and to Alec Bodkin, Richard Gipps, Kelso Cratsley, and Philosophy and Education Research Association-members Jane Roland Martin, Janet Farrell Smith, Barbara Houston, Ann Diller, Beatrice Kipp Nelson and Susan Fransoza, each of whom read parts of the manuscript in draft form. As always, my best editor was Frank Keefe.

If some man in Bedlam should entertain you with sober discourse, says Hobbes, and ". . . you desire that you might another time requite his civility; and he should tell you, he were God the father; I think you need expect no extravagant action for argument of his Madnesse."[1]

His sober discourse and civility count for nothing, the absurdity of this one notion seals Hobbes's judgement: the man is delusional, and mad. The conviction that he is God is the antithesis of reasoned good sense, its patent falsity tied to its ungroundedness – the fact that there could be no reasons, or at least none Hobbes could imagine, that might warrant such a conviction.

These ideas concern rationality and reasonableness, how it is right and appropriate to acquire, hold and integrate beliefs and belief-like states, and they are our immediate concern here. But the concept of delusion is a complex and highly charged one, embodying ingredients that are social and medical as well. Ideas about how beliefs are properly held shape how delusions are understood; so, too, do conceptions of behavioral rationality assessing how beliefs are realized in action. Mental health lore (and law) deem to be irrational behavior that is self destructive, for example, and assign negative value to other responses that are socially, communicatively and occupationally limiting.

The strange notions entertained by madmen have consistently provided a foil against which the proper way to reason is recognized and defined. Delusion is a category shaped by these values, I think it can be shown, and the concept of delusion is saturated with ideas about how cognitive judgements are *properly* achieved. Moral values are also involved when we speak of the way delusions are held, and the actions stemming from them. But the values that are our initial concern here are epistemic, rather than moral. They involve evaluative judgements about how we believe and know.

TERMS EMPLOYED

Extended and metaphorical uses of "delusion" and its cognates abound ("She's delusional if she thinks we can get by without raising taxes"; "He has deluded himself into the belief he's attractive to her," and so on); they are an indication of the centrality of delusion to our conception of ourselves as believers and knowers. Such uses can be set to one side. Our interest is solely in the "delusions" of clinical and research discourses. Even in those we find no consistent language though, and terms mired in ambiguity and even circularity. For instance, hallucinations and delusions are usually identified as the hallmarks of psychosis. Yet if all delusional thought is deemed psychotic, as it is on some reckonings, clinical delusions are not helpfully differentiated as products of psychosis. And adding to the confusion, some have spoken of "benign psychosis" to describe states of delusion and hallucination lacking uncomfortable, or otherwise disabling aspects for those who experience them.[2]

The expression "pathological delusions" is little better. It introduces contested presuppositions about the nature of disease and illness. The presumption that brain deficiencies explain and serve to sharply separate all true delusions from more commonplace errors of reason and judgement, for example, while perhaps true, is − thus far − less than fully established. Hypothesized it may be, but it cannot be taken for granted. Nor can the model by which delusions are deemed part of the symptom cluster of a particular, distinct, underlying disease process.

In this book, the term "clinical delusion" is used for the category that others have entitled "true," "psychotic" or "pathological" delusions. Those whose delusions are a source of distress or danger to themselves or other people are likely those seen in the clinic, and on that basis the expression was selected. "Clinical delusions" has its problems and limitations as well (including the obvious misidentifications to be expected from misleading patients and inept practitioners). But it would be unwarranted to assume that true delusions belong to any unitary natural category, distinguishable by kind. Singling out those more severe and disabling delusional states with the term "clinical delusions" this way helps remind the reader that delusions are in this discussion presumed to be no more than "practical" kinds (Zachar): they are members of a class whose commonality lies with immediate, practical human concerns − which are in this instance those of the clinical setting.

Doubtless some delusions of the kind discussed in these chapters occur outside the clinic. Even people with dangerous "clinical" delusions will sometimes avoid the treatment and care they need. (When they find a belief community among their followers, delusional leaders seem to be "insulated" by charismatic personality, for example.[3]) And some people whose beliefs violated political rather than mental health norms have been subject to clinical treatment. (Whether the clinical deprograming of former jihadists promoted by the Kingdom of Saudi Arabia fits this last category is for the reader to decide.)

THEMES

Rationality and reasonableness are understood to be normative in the present discussion: they reflect ideals and values.[4] In contrast, some of the epistemic ingredients embodied in conceptions of delusion express statistical norms – determining what we could expect. And while what is (statistically) normal often matches what is normative, the two sometimes diverge. Normal reasoners and rational agents are imperfect reasoners and rational agents. They are prone to any number of reasoning biases, for example, engendering flawed judgement. (Confirmation bias is one of these, i.e., a tendency to select and interpret evidence to confirm preconceived ideas.)

By emphasizing the normative ingredients in the concept of delusion, this account diverges from much contemporary research, where the broader cultural meanings within which delusions are embedded are for the most part ignored. Acknowledgement of those broader cultural meanings provides a reminder – and a respectful rebalancing – in relation to that neglect.

The analysis in this book is in line with one strand of contemporary research. The reasoning strategies employed by delusional and normal subjects are readily compared, and have struck some studying them more by their similarities than their differences.[5] Thus, attention has been directed away from florid clinical states, and instead toward their margins. Michel Foucault's elegiac history of madness, depicting delusional states as indistinguishable from everyday folly and foolishness during the pre-modern era, may be exaggerated.

Nonetheless, intermediate states that formed a penumbra around clinical delusions have long been recognized by clinical observers. In particular, these states did not go unnoticed in early twentieth-century taxonomies. There, "delusion-like" and "overvalued" ideas were regularly described: dubiously warranted and unlikely convictions and preoccupations that closely resemble (and often accompany) more florid clinical delusions.[6]

Quasi-delusional and delusion-like states have sometimes received recognition as delusional; at other times the class of delusions proper has been pruned to exclude them. (In his *General Psychopathology* [1997/1913] Karl Jaspers took the latter approach.) Clinical and research writing continues to reflect this tension: sometimes true or proper delusions are segregated along Jasperian lines; in other instances, "delusion" includes the milder, intermediate states as well. More particularly, too, belief states associated with some conditions (such as eating disorders) are tossed back and forth, judged to be delusions proper in one discussion, and merely delusion-like (or forms of overvalued ideas), in another.

More obvious than these intermediate states that seem to fall between extreme delusions and normal states is another aspect of the clinical phenomena: the diversity of features exhibited among even incontestable cases of delusion. The variations and differences here are striking, belying any model by which a bulwark of central cases *sharing all features* gives way to variations within a gray area at its periphery. Rather than comprising a uniform core, clinical delusions form a heterogeneous assemblage. Loosely sorted into different kinds of delusions, it can perhaps be. But only with considerable oversimplification can that assemblage be seen as one phenomenon, rather than a miscellany. The sheer *range and variety* of states that arguably fall within the loose category of clinical delusions form one of the central demonstrations of this book.

For the most part, recent discussions by theorists and practitioners have been narrowly focused, eschewing consideration of the broader group. They have paid attention almost exclusively to two kinds of phenomena, moreover: the simple ("monothematic") conditions associated with neurological disease and damage to the brain, and the delusional states of schizophrenia. Yet delusions are associated with almost every kind of major mental disorder: particular delusions of grandeur, of guilt, of possession, of infestation, of persecution, of jealousy, and so on. They are linked to a broad range of diagnoses as well – schizophrenia and the eponymous "delusional disorders," but also mood disorders and some character and dissociative conditions, as well as a host of neurological syndromes. If these diagnostic categories are themselves valid, then delusions are in this respect somewhat comparable to raised body temperature in ordinary medicine – a widely occurring symptom of many unrelated disorders.

The narrow research attention of the first decade of the twenty-first century has had the effect of neglecting many complex ("polythematic") delusions, including many commonly found in the clinic, and by way of redress, some of these other kinds of delusion are emphasized in the present work. But quite apart from this neglect, there seems to be a risk to the piecemeal approach of most contemporary research. Without considering clinical delusions *together*, we may fail to recognize the heterogeneities involved and the variety of ways these phenomena stray from norms of rationality, reasonableness, coherence and common sense.

Such limited focus also offers short shrift when it comes to the conceptual tasks of definition and characterization. Some researchers explicitly avoid conclusions about *all* delusions on the basis of what they have discovered about some, or some kinds. Others proceed on the apparent assumption that broad types of delusion are each separate kinds, better examined, and defined, separately. Certainly attempts at a definition sweeping enough to cover all clinical delusions have consistently met with failure, beset by exceptions. But if these analyses are so limited, we might wonder why little research has been devoted to the matter of how these different kinds of delusion relate to one another, if they do at all.

Some of the range and variety of clinical delusions seen in the psychiatric clinic will be introduced in Chapter 2, and one example within this miscellany, because it will likely seem anomalous, deserves some preliminary explanation. Psychiatry has always recognized *folies à deux*, where delusional ideas initially acquired by one person are spread to an intimate. But to the evidence acknowledging *folies à deux* (and *à trois*, and even *à famille*), must be added a history documenting delusions that are solely, or primarily, the product of less intimate social interaction.

Granted, few such epidemics probably indicate mental disorder, let alone clinical delusion. In *Memoirs of Extraordinary Popular Delusions* (1841), Charles Mackay describes his compilation of "the most remarkable instances of these moral epidemics which have been excited," his aim to show "how easily the masses have been led astray, and how imitative and gregarious men are. . . ." Popular delusions, he notes "began so early, spread so widely, and have lasted so long, that instead of two or three volumes, fifty would scarcely suffice to detail their history."[7]

Whether our examples come from the financial markets, as some of Mackay's did, from popular political movements such as National Socialism, or from the Internet, and whether or not we dignify them with the name *delusions*, Mackay is right that innumerable false and foolish ideas spread with a speed and readiness that bespeaks some sort of social contagion. They are certainly not all, or not perhaps often, clinical states. But in some cases, they are. When delusional ideas are acquired in a process that bypasses normal and reasonable forms of social learning, and are associated with behavioral epidemics of self destructiveness (eating disorders, and self-mutilation, for example) they are seen in the clinic. So they deserve their place in our inventory.

The view that delusions differ in degree rather than kind from more ordinary errors is a difficult one to overturn not merely because the evidence in its favor is persuasive. The presence of this shading from clinical delusions to more normal states does not resolve this question, nor does the heterogeneity of delusions seen in the clinic, I will contend in Chapter 3. The burden of proof may rest with those who hold that delusions are different in kind, not with those denying it, nonetheless. For this matter is not solely methodological. It is also moral and cultural: centuries of using delusional thinking to separate those with such disorder from the epistemic, moral and even human community, seem to encourage *starting with inclusion*. And emphasizing the commonalities between delusions and everyday errors, rather than the differences dividing them, would seem to better honor that approach. (We'll see [Chapter 4] the same uneven burden arguably falls on those attributing meaninglessness or incomprehensibility to clinical delusions. Some delusions do appear to be meaningless and incomprehensible, but the default presumption must be that they make sense.)

Delusions have been the focus of widely divergent interpretations by theorists, so it may be useful to state at the outset what is not countenanced here. The apparent continuum uniting clinical delusions with more everyday errors of judgement might be supposed to indicate the skeptical conclusion that delusional phenomena reflect reasoning that is *different*, rather than intrinsically *flawed*. This is not a position entertained in the following pages. Whatever uncertainties surround how delusions are to be understood, it is presumed they represent, at their extreme, serious dysfunction appropriately treated in a clinical setting. Presupposed here, moreover, is that the class of clinical delusions is some sort of grouping deserving investigation.

Delusion is a loose ("folk psychological") category, granted, and findings in brain science, cognitive psychology, or treatment, may one day encourage us to reduce the class of true clinical delusions, excluding some hitherto located within this miscellany. Presently, in grouping these states together, we must rely on the trained and sensitive judgement of clinicians. Fortunately, it seems to be judgement we are entitled to trust.[8] Treating clinical delusions may be challenging, but identifying them, apparently, is not.

The chapters that follow are linked by themes, rather than proceeding systematically. That delusions are entwined with epistemic values about the proper way to acquire, maintain and integrate beliefs is the first of these themes, and some of the cultural background of these ideas is provided in Chapter 1. Delusions have been central emblems of irrationality and unreasonableness, used as a heuristic for understanding not only illogic and incomprehensibility, but skepticism and solipsism. As such, they have played an undisputed part in (Western) philosophy of the modern period. With these uses, however, has come an impenetrable and distorting binary system serving to place all delusional thinking at a polar remove from sanity. Delusions, and the minds and madness with which they are associated, have represented otherness (*alterity*), and exclusion from the epistemic and human community. Although they are *also* observable clinical phenomena, delusions thus embody cultural meaning and associations that influence how they are understood, both by those who observe them, and by their unfortunate subjects.

The undeniably exciting and fruitful work on delusions undertaken during the last two decades within philosophy, cognitive psychology, and brain science has stimulated further themes.[9] First, although much can be learned from this research, fundamental uncertainties remain, and debates persist, about how delusions are to be understood. Whether a difference in kind or degree distinguishes clinical *delusions* from more everyday misinterpretations and from the plethora of erroneous, strongly valued, ill-grounded, unproven, or unprovable ideas, beliefs and attitudes to which ordinary people often cling tenaciously, is one of these questions. The nature of the relation between different types of delusion, noted above, is another. (What do the particular, limited delusions resulting from brain damage and disease tell us about the elaborate delusional *belief systems* of paranoia, for example?) There is also the question of whether delusions are always – or ever – beliefs. Can attitudes, moods, values and desires be delusional? Are delusions mistakenly *confused with* genuine beliefs? And what kinds of causal explanation can be expected to shed light on them? (Agreement over none of these questions has been reached, and the uncertainties surrounding them are introduced in Chapter 3.)

A second group of questions raised in contemporary research involves the meaningfulness of delusional assertions (Chapter 4). They are usually expressed in grammatically faultless language, but are these assertions always, or ever, about matters that *make sense* to the observer, or even to their subject? And can influential theories of meaning drawn from philosophers like Wittgenstein and Davidson help answer that question? One of these theories seems to encourage us to attribute meaningfulness to delusional ideas *even when they elude comprehensibility*. Another equates meaning with intersubjective agreement, so that meaningfulness can be seen as *reducing to* being understood by others.

Two related ideas emerge from the discussion of these matters: that many fundamental questions remain, and that these sweeping accounts of meaning may be too powerful for the multidimensional nature of clinical delusions, which apparently *vary* with respect to their meaningfulness and comprehensibility (as they do with respect to much else). From the number of hypotheses canvassed by contemporary research, moreover, it is possible to conclude that one size will not fit all when it comes to understanding delusions. The diverse analyses and hypotheses may reflect less the creativity of observers' imaginations and the ambiguity of their subject matter – although each of these is considerable – than the range and variety within the sprawling category of delusions itself.

Accounts of delusional states as idiosyncratic, even solipsistic, introduce another theme (discussed in Chapter 4): delusions can be both shared and unshared. Against the *unshared* nature of meanings, associated with some delusions, are placed delusions which are *shared*, including the *folies à deux* traditionally recognized in psychiatry, and the group contagions by which some disordered beliefs, attitudes and behavioral tendencies seem to spread (introduced in Chapter 5). This issue also raises the special epistemic status of delusions that are religious, spiritual, metaphysical and ideological, and the fact that when widely shared, some religious belief seems to be exempted from rational scrutiny (Chapter 6). Efforts to distinguish normal religious belief from delusions with religious themes demand special attention, I stress, because such ideas and such delusions are linked to dangerous and violent action.

Delusions introduce moral as well as other values, and this is the final theme. The effects of delusions on the person understood first as an *epistemic*, and then a *moral*, agent are the focus of Chapters 7 and 8. How should we assess someone in light of his delusions, or judge his adherence to them? What philosophers call epistemic virtues generate obligations about how we acquire, maintain and integrate our ideas. And these obligations arguably extend to delusional subjects as well. In a person who possesses the insight and self-control to adhere to them, how must we assess neglect of such obligations? When delusions are the attributes of groups and deemed "social contagion," what is the moral status of responses resulting from their spread? Delusions also shape character and frame motivation. What, then, are we to make of seemingly delusional self-assessments – of grandiosity, vanity and undue self-denigration? Grandiose delusions, particularly, seem to merge imperceptibly into the personality trait of grandiosity and from there to the sin of pride. How do we square clinical and moral discourses, if so? (This is discussed in Chapter 7.) And finally (Chapter 8), delusions sometimes direct action.

How are dangerous deeds such as those of the violent maniac and the religious or ideological zealot to be evaluated when they result from delusional thinking?

We learn about clinical delusions from two main sources, each imperfect: case records of what their patients have told clinicians, and the written material, including memoirs, provided by the patients themselves. Due to the elusive, often ineffable nature of what so many delusions are over or about, and the seemingly strange manner in which they are often adhered to, finding out about and describing delusional states when they occur in others is not an easy task, however skilled, patient and empathic the inquirer. Some of the same limitations will accompany first-person accounts – added to which, those accounts often come to us after the fact, re-conceived as the result of forgetting, recast from shame, abhorrence, and newly minted perspectives, and, in the case of those that reach the status of literary works, imaginative reinvention.[10] In spite of these drawbacks, my money is on first-person accounts, and I have relied on them wherever possible to illustrate the mental states we are interested in. The nature of delusions rests not only with their content, and how they were acquired and are maintained, but in how they fit within their subject's broader frame of mind, behavior and history. Detail and subtlety are needed in such an inquiry as in few others, and the best of these first-hand accounts offer us detail and subtlety that is unmatched. We need others' cooperation to find out what they are experiencing in clinical practice just as we do in everyday life, as Jaspers has observed, and an experience is best described "by the person who has undergone it."[11]

First-hand descriptions are not immune from the presuppositions and preoccupations of their own time and place, and to see beyond the effects of such "local" framing, examples were sought from earlier as well as contemporary times. In addition, I have where possible used those clinical descriptions dating from the unhurried era of the great asylums. It was a time when patients were observed for months and years, rather than days, and clinicians recorded their observations with an extraordinary attention to detail.

RATIONALE

Clinical delusions have practical and social importance that compels us to understand them. Not only are they used to identify the severe mental disorder that excuses in the criminal law; they trigger any number of protections, exceptions and special arrangements enshrined in other social policy, and reflected in everyday moral assessments. The primary goal of the following pages, then, is clarificatory. Insufficiently understood, delusion has a central place in our, and perhaps every, society. It behoves us to look more closely at the tangle of cultural meanings, values and psychopathology making up the category (or categories) of delusion.

One

The imaginative grip of modernist epistemology affects our seeing and being in the world in incalculable ways. Framing philosophical thought since Descartes, madness and delusion are emblematic of this influence, providing a foil for analyses of knowledge, belief, rationality and sound reasoning, and helping to demarcate philosophical skepticism. But the influence has been reciprocal and iterative. This role in the theory of knowledge has in turn affected conceptions of madness and disorder, framing the very categories by which we know them. The location of delusion at the center of severe mental disorder reflects a legacy, arguably traceable to Greek philosophical ideas, and certainly integral to modernist thought, whereby the very essence of humanity lies with our ability to reason. As this suggests, one of the most vital foci in Western thinking, at least in modern times, has been this nexus where delusion, madness and rationality meet.

What follows is a series of extended examples drawn from influential philosophical writing of the modern era. By seeing delusion placed in contrast to epistemic norms of sound reasoning and good sense, and madmen excluded from membership in an epistemic community, we glimpse some of the complex associations that form an inescapable part of present-day conceptions of both reason and its absence. And similarly, by recognizing the way madness has been identified with qualities that are morally and socially disvalued – the bodily and bestial, the feminine, the diabolical, for example – we see its further links with otherness and exclusion. Influenced by Foucault, contemporary writing goes further than I do here. That writing traces the implications of these connections to paradox, and to the transformation of the voices of the mad speaking of their own states to mute incomprehensibility. However, even the brief review provided in this chapter will be sufficient to demonstrate how, as the antithesis of reason, delusion reflects, and is reflected, in it.

DESCARTES

Madmen and their delusions enter modern philosophy with Descartes's first moments of doubt in the *Meditations*. Considering sensory evidence in more sweeping terms, he at first finds some certainty, although certainty that is short-lived, in beliefs about what is immediately before him – his hands, and body. Later, remembering the distortions that occur in dreams, he will despair of trusting even this seemingly most immediate and incontrovertible knowledge. But to establish a contrast for that seeming, albeit temporary, certainty, Descartes at this opening moment in his meditation, introduces "certain lunatics [Latin *amentes*]" (Descartes 1960/1641). The brains of these victims of strange and powerful delusions, he asserts, are

> . . . so befogged by the black vapors of the bile that they continually affirm that they are kings while they are paupers; that they are clothed [in gold] and purple while they are naked; or imagine that their head is made of clay, or that they are gourds, or that their body is glass.

In contrast to these madmen's thoughts, he implies, and at least over the most intimate and immediate evidence about his physical person – his own senses are to be trusted. He can see his hands, his limbs. He would be judged to be a madman himself were he to doubt these claims[1] – ". . . such men are fools, and I would be no less insane [*demens*] than they if I followed their example."

The humoral disorder of melancholia, to which Descartes alludes in this passage, was an encompassing category. It included the deficiencies of imagination and judgement we today recognize as delusional thought. And Descartes's description echoes accounts of such humoral disorders from the learned Low Countries doctors of his time, two of whose works were almost certainly known to him. André Du Laurens (1560?–1609) was one. His authoritative review of medical thought from Galen onwards, gathered in *Discours de la conservation de la veue: Des maladies melancholiques: des catarrhs: & de la vieillesse* (*Discourse on the Preservation of Sight: of Melancholike Diseases, of Rheumes, and of Old Age*) (1597) and printed in Latin as well as French editions, remained influential into well on in the seventeenth century. The other was Felix Platter (1536–1614), author of an influential textbook, *Praxeos Medicae*, published in the first of several editions in 1602, and much quoted throughout the seventeenth and even eighteenth centuries.

Du Laurens defines melancholia as a kind of "dotage" without fever; in such a condition "some one of the principall faculties of the minde, as imagination or reason is corrupted." When this occurs, the sufferer is "assayled with a thousand vaine visions, and hideous buggards, with fantasticall inventions, and dreadfull dreames. . . ." All "melancholike" persons, he remarks "have their imagination troubled . . . and often have their reason corrupted as well." This effect results from the melancholy humor, or black bile, "a cold and drie distemperature of the braine." The humor's coldness and blackness affect the "animal spirits," which in turn affect the faculties of the mind "principally the imagination, presenting unto it continually black formes and strange visions." (These passages are quoted in S. Jackson 1986: 87–8.)

Platter's account is very similar. Melancholy, he says, named from black bile, is a kind of mental alienation (*mentis alienatio*) in which imagination and judgement are so perverted that without any cause the melancholy sufferers cannot adduce any certain cause of grief or fear except a trivial one or a false opinion, "conceived as a result of disturbed apprehension. . . ." And others, "deceive themselves with some other nonsense conceived in and impressed on their minds, like the man who thought he had become an earthenware vessel and gave way to everyone and everything he met, fearing that he would collide with them. Thus, some believe that they are turned into brute animals . . . Others talk foolishly that they have devoured serpents or frogs and are bearing them alive in their bodies, or have other delusions; they talk foolishly of many such marvelous things." (This passage is from Diethelm and Heffernan 1965: 15.)

By Descartes's era, the ancient humoral explanations of delusional states were giving way to more "scientific" references to the movement of animal spirits, as we see in the passage from Du Laurens, above. While still commonplace, humoral descriptions such as Descartes's with its reference to dark, bilious vapors, were invoked more for their metaphorical than explanatory value. And indeed, by the time he writes *The Passions of the Soul* (1649), all reference to dark, bilious vapors arising from "adusted" (overheated) black bile has disappeared and Descartes, also, introduces the language of animal spirits.

The delusions of madmen lead Descartes to consider dreams. In dreams, he admits, he can entertain ideas as improbable and unreal as those of the madman. And again, the contrast: he admits to "imagin[ing] the same things that lunatics imagine when awake, or sometimes things which are even less plausible." This very observation is to be repeated by Kant. The lunatic, he remarks, is "a dreamer in the waking state." What the madman experiences and believes in come to other men only during sleep. (Later though, we shall see, Kant gets beyond this unhelpful way of characterizing the distinction.)

And if all experience is like dreams? This unsettling possibility, Descartes now acknowledges. Yet he does not return to revise or correct his previous contrast between the waking delusions of madmen, and the sleeping illusions of the sane. Instead he moves on, to find passing comfort in generality and abstraction, and in the goodness of his Creator, before imagining an even more alarming possibility: he might be the victim of a powerful malevolent force intent on misleading him ("a certain evil spirit, not less clever and deceitful than powerful [who] has bent all his efforts to deceiving me"). Nothing, by the end of the first day of meditation, will dispel "the darkness of all the difficulties which have just been raised." The deceiving demon now envisioned might have "employed all his artifice to deceive me" so that everything – "the sky, the air, the earth, colors, shapes, sounds, and all other objective things, are nothing but illusions and dreams, that he has used to trick my credulity."

Imagining a force so powerful, so malignant, so unsettling, so destructive of his prized power of reason – now Descartes sounds like a madman himself. If the delusions of madmen are like the illusions of sane men's dreams, as he has previously admitted, and a deceiving demon renders all belief to such a state of uncertainty, then indeed, there can be nothing to separate sane men's beliefs from madmen's delusions. The general knowledge Descartes has earlier demonstrated about the effects of the vapors on the disordered imagination might encourage us to expect he would recognize this, and say so. But he does not.

The madman who believes such a devilish plot was a standard part of medical description and as well known as the pitiably deluded sufferers Descartes had earlier alluded to, who deemed themselves monarchs when they were in the greatest poverty, or made of clay, glass or gourds. Under the same encompassing category of melancholia, whose humoral effects on the brain Descartes depicted at the outset of his meditation, certain case descriptions have recurred since ancient times. He who complains of being the subject of others' ill-intended attention and malice was familiar from classical, as well as medieval and Renaissance accounts. The very same descriptions that provided Descartes with his detailed depiction of those dark, bilious vapors, also dwell on such encompassing paranoid delusions. Du Laurens speaks of the melancholike man as always fearful, trembling, afraid of everything, and subject to a consuming watchfulness, asleep and awake, so that he is "assailed with a thousand vaine visions, and hideous buggards with fantasticall inventions, and dreadfull dreames." (Quoted in S. Jackson 1986: 87.) But Descartes seems reluctant to acknowledge this similarity. The madman has been positioned in polar opposite to the inquiring philosopher, and even that philosopher's insanest doubts are different – because they stand in contrast to the perorations of the madman.

Kant's ideas on delusions are to be found in a section of the *Anthropology from a Pragmatic Point of View*, the late work drawn from his lecture notes at the very end of the eighteenth century. Although brief, these passages are revealing for the seemingly original and non-medical taxonomy on the different ways the cognitive capacities might be impaired, and Kant is in several ways the hero of the present philosophical excursion. There is the "tumultuous" madness (*amentia*) seen in the garrulous women in the madhouse; the "methodical" insanity (*dementia*) resulting from a falsely inventive imagination, where "self-concocted ideas" are treated as if they were accurate perceptions; delirium (*insania*), described as the only fragmentarily methodical flights of those whose minds are deceived by analogies; and finally, there is lunacy (*vesania*) which, although "systematic," reveals a complete disregard for the facts of experience. This last, Kant describes not just as lack of reason, but as positive unreason.

In part differentiated from one another by differences of degree, these categories, together with his inventory of the various forms of unreason and foolishness, might lead us to expect that Kant understood the differences between insanity and foolishness to be dimensional matters, of degree rather than kind. Yet it seems not. For as he says, the simpleton, the coxcomb, the stupid, the imprudent, the fool and the buffoon are all different from the mentally disordered ". . . not merely in degree but in the distinctive quality of mental discord." Despite their failings, these people do not belong in a madhouse, he insists. Fanaticism, superstition and eccentricity each affect the cognitive faculty as well, yet they too are radically different from madness.

Having set aside these lesser forms of cognitive defect, Kant goes on to speak of the distinguishing feature of the true insanity with which they have been placed in contrast. The only general characteristic of that condition, he asserts, is that there is a replacement of ideas "common to all" (*sensus communis*) by those ideas that are "peculiar to ourselves" (*sensus privatus*) leading to judgements that are indiosyncratic, and subjective.[2] Then, in terms that prefigure nothing so much as the later Wittgenstein, Kant explains that agreement in judgement between people, only achieved through checking with them (or reading books) guarantees the "objectivity" of those judgements. The madman, because of his failure (or his inability) to check for agreement with others in reaching his judgements, is trapped in a "merely subjective" understanding. For it is

> . . . a subjectively necessary touchstone of the correctness of our judgement and, consequently, of the soundness of our understanding that we relate our understanding to the understanding of others, and not merely isolate ourselves within our own experiences. . . .
>
> (Kant 1978: 117)

Intersubjective agreement, then, is the basis of "objectivity" for Kant, i.e., correct judgement and sound understanding. And it is this necessary touchstone for the correctness of judgement and the soundness of our understanding, as he puts it, that the madman has lost.

As well as a precursor of Wittgenstein's ideas, Kant's reference to a lack of objectivity in delusional judgements may be seen as a harbinger of more recent psychiatric lore. If Kant's notion of objectivity can be equated with that of "reality," then this passage seems to be recognizable in the claim that the delusions and hallucinations marking psychosis show a want of "reality-testing." (With regard to this equation, we must note that Kant's ambiguous metaphysics around external reality is the source of continuing and unresolved controversy among his philosophical interpreters. And perhaps we can suppose that, speaking for a more general audience and towards the end of his life, Kant himself chose his terms in the lectures that comprised his *Anthropologie* to retain, rather than resolve, this ambiguity. It may be more, but at the least object-ivity is a reflection of intersubjective agreement, in this account. And so, arguably, is reality understood in the "reality-testing" criterion in contemporary psychiatric practice.)

The examples Kant provides in these passages involve per-ception: when a man "hears a voice no-one else hears." Later, as we would expect from his recognition that some forms of madness involve speculations entirely removed from experi-ence, he speaks of judgements about less immediately per-ceptual matters. Someone who does not bother with the touchstone, but "gets it into his head to acknowledge his own private opinion as already valid without regard for, or even against, common opinion," Kant explains, has "submitted to a play of thoughts in which he proceeds and judges in a world not shared with other people, but rather (as in a dream) he sees himself in his own world." (These and earlier quoted passages are from §§50–3 of the *Anthropologie*.) Trapped in experiences as detached, erroneous and solipsistic as those of the dreamer, all madmen are alike doomed to unsound judgement and flawed understanding.

SCHOPENHAUER

Schopenhauer (1788–1860) provides us with a third philosophical use of the delusions of madmen to establish rationality norms and the bounds of epistemology. *The World as Will and Idea* emphasizes the contrast between the world of appearances to which positivistic science is limited, and an "external" world that goes beyond our own ideas (and will) and that is somehow known to us subjectively, through the effects of our embodiment and our sense of agency. With other metaphysical idealists, Schopenhauer at first recognizes the limits imposed by our access to appearances. But using a refined, metaphysical concept of will, linked to embodiment, he attempts to show how we can go beyond them to the underlying ("noumenal") realities of which they are appearances.

The success of Schopenhauer's project need not concern us. In resisting the notion that what exists can be captured in what is perceived (*esse est percipi*), however, Schopenhauer introduces the possibility, and specter, of solipsism – the position that only myself or modifications of myself exist, and that other human beings exist solely as my ideas. To embrace this position, he asserts, must be to engage in delusional thinking: it is akin to madness.

Adopting a solipsistic metaphysics such as this (Schopenhauer's term for it is "theoretical egoism") Schopenhauer explains in *The World as Will and Idea* (1995/1818), the person must assume of his object of perception that it "is essentially different from all others." For ". . . it alone of all objects is at once both will and idea, while the rest are only ideas, i.e., only phantoms." The person must then assume "that his body is the only real individual in the world i.e. the only phenomenon of will and the only immediate object of the subject." The real meaning of the question as to the reality of the external world, Schopenhauer then explains, draws us towards theoretical egoism that "holds all phenomena, excepting its own individual self to be phantoms. . . ." It is a position, he admits, which can never be proven false. Yet in philosophy, "it has never been used other than as a skeptical sophism, i.e., only for show." As a serious conviction, on the other hand, "it could be found *only in a madhouse*, and as such it would need not so much a refutation as a cure" (pp. 36–7, emphasis added). (Others have also attributed solipsism to the strangely idiosyncratic "private" language employed by the madman, and it is a subject to which we'll return in Chapter 4.)

Thus satisfied, Schopenhauer moves on. We need concern ourselves with theoretical egoism no further, he concludes. Theoretically, as "the last bastion of skepticism, which is always polemical," it is irrefutable. (Quoted passages are from a 2002 edn, pp. 36–7.) But it is incompatible with reason and common sense. Only the madman could accept the possibility of theoretical egoism; for the rest of us it must be regarded as a philosophical feint. And cure, rather than refutation, marks the proper response to such delusions.

Schopenhauer reached these conclusions after some clinical exploration. Between 1811 and 1813, and thus before the 1819 publication of *The World as Will and Idea*, he observed and became acquainted with psychiatric patients in the Berlin Charité Hospital. Explaining this investigation, he has said "Nowhere did I find a clear and satisfactory explanation of the nature of madness . . . Thus, I had to search for such information in the madhouses myself . . ." (quoted by Zentner 2002: 373).[3] Schopenhauer is not offering a clinical description in his philosophical work, however. Rather, the madman is introduced as a foil. Theoretical egoism (solipsism) is not a position it is possible for rational beings to truly believe. Only the madman, who will believe anything, could adopt it. But he is excluded. For all the seemingly irrefutable coherence of the position attributed to him, the madman is no longer a member of the epistemic community.

WITTGENSTEIN

Wittgenstein's *On Certainty*, written in the last years before his death in 1951, is a repudiation of Descartes's program of systematic doubt. Here, the doubts of madmen are emblems of the mistaken approaches that have misled philosophers and philosophy. Yet Wittgenstein also uses madness and delusion throughout that and other work to provide a contrast, a foil, a code for otherness, difference and incomprehensibility.

To appreciate this contrast, we need to understand the position explored by Wittgenstein in this small, late work of numbered observations. First, he is setting forth a kind of holism. No one belief can be treated – or doubted – in isolation. ("What I hold fast to is not one proposition but a nest of propositions"; 1969: §225) And doubt must come to an end. (Must I not begin to trust somewhere, he asks? "That is to say: somewhere I must begin with not-doubting . . ."; §150). Wittgenstein is deriding the philosophers' exercise of systematic doubt. Therein, he suggests, lies delusion and madness. The very idea that each individual belief is supported by grounds is for Wittgenstein a misapprehension, moreover. There are many beliefs, including many empirical beliefs ("an hour ago this table existed," for example), that cannot be doubted, he insistently asserts – or rather, that only a madman would doubt.

More generally, delusions are not to be understood as explained in terms of reasons at all. Rather, they are the brute by-products of a disordered brain – brought about by causes, rather than reasons. What is the difference between mistake and mental disturbance, Wittgenstein asks (§71) –

". . . a mistake doesn't only have a cause, it also has a ground, i.e., roughly, when someone makes a mistake, this can be fitted into what he knows aright" (§74). This ground, or background, where reason-giving is practiced, and within which even mistakes can be understood, is absent for those with mental disorder.

In modern Western philosophy at least, this sampling of passages illustrates, the delusions of madmen are not so much considered in their own right as used for contrast – with what it is rational to believe, with how, and how far it is possible to doubt, and with what must be privileged as certain, true and known. Delusions provide the limiting case, and margin, the contrary or polar opposite, of reason, reasoning, rationality and shared meanings, of the perorations that take place in the "space of reasons," and of the rational community. Arguably, Kant does better than this in his analysis of the difference between the insane and the rest of us. Although tantalizingly brief, his are reasoned categories. But Kant too, presupposes the vast gulf excluding the madman from all others.

Since Foucault's influential writing about the history of madness, a standard trope has emerged: the madman as Other. And just as theorizing has unveiled the cultural meanings or "structures" that assign women and the feminine to deficiency and perversion, as well as to madness, so madness has been understood to be part of a symbolic economy. Here, it is all that is contrary not only to our ideals of rationality, reason, community and meaningfulness, but to other valued human attributes.

These ideas have been treated with care and thoroughness by several contemporary theorists and are noted only briefly here.[4] They have also been the source of far-reaching conclusions that will not all be embraced in the present discussion. Two aspects of this body of scholarship about madness by, or inspired by, Michel Foucault are sufficient to make our case: the long associative link between delusions and an extensive range of disvalued qualities and attributes other than those noted thus far, and the misrepresentation and stereotyping that have attended that cluster of associations.

Whether or not the otherness of madness has its origins in ancient Greek notions of *logos*, with madness set against rational self-consciousness, as has been claimed, more modern times introduced new polarities.[5] By the era when Descartes and Du Laurens are writing about delusion, madness had been tied to the bodily, the feminine, carnal and bestial, to black magic, and social disorder, among other things. A passage by Du Laurens illustrates the link with bestiality. Consider the action of a frenetic or a maniac, he remarks, "*you'll find nothing human there*: he bites, he screams, he bellows with a savage voice, rolls burning eyes, his hair stands on end, he throws himself about and often kills himself so." (Emphasis added. This passage is translated by Thiher 2002: 74.)

As the Other, delusional madness is not only disvalued but misunderstood, the object of stereotyped apprehension and overgeneralization. Sander Gilman speaks of the categories into which visual stereotypes can be divided as reflecting

> . . . certain basic perceptual categories, which are in turn projections of internalized, often repressed models of the self and the Other . . . the categories of difference reflect our preoccupation with the self and the control that the self must have over the world.

Of all the models of pathology, he observes, one of the most powerful is mental illness. And what is perceived is "in large part a projection":

> . . . the mad are perceived as the antithesis to the control and reason that define the self. . . . This is not to say that mental illness does not exist . . . but that the function of the idea of mental illness within the sign system of our mental representations shapes our "seeing the insane."
>
> (Gilman 1985: 23–4)

The associative link between delusions and other disvalued qualities, and the misrepresentation that comes with the binary distinction between valued categories and otherness that Gilman observes, are all we require to support the claim illustrated earlier in this chapter by reference to particular, influential remarks from the modern epistemological tradition. Delusion is a category framed, and distorted, by its relation to reason. Added to these ways madness and delusion have been cast as the antithesis of all we value, find sensible, and even human, moreover, has been the more concrete evidence of social exclusion documented by historians. As the Other, madmen were removed to the limits of actual society as well as the limits of cultural meaning.

Combining these two factors – cultural meanings and the evidence of actual mistreatment and exclusion – some theorists have drawn several more ambitious and broader conclusions. The first asserts that, after the age of reason, madmen were "reduced to silence," their voices no longer heard. Dialogue between madness and reason thus precluded, the language of psychiatry could be nothing more than a "monologue" of reason about madness. As Foucault puts it in a much quoted preface to his *History of Madness* (2006/1961) his aim was to uncover the "archeology" of the silence to which madness had been reduced.

But paradox and impossibility reside in the very goal Foucault sets himself, and that is the second, related concern. What has been silenced cannot be heard, after all. The task laid out in his history of madness is, as Foucault himself says, impossible, even "doubly impossible":

> . . . it would have us reconstitute the dust of actual suffering, of senseless words . . . and especially since that suffering and those words can only exist and be offered to themselves and to others in an act of division which already denounces and masters them . . . The perception which seeks to seize them in their natural state belongs necessarily to a world which has already captured them.
>
> (Preface xxxii)

We need not adopt either of these additional conclusions to accept much that such theories have explained. As emblematic of otherness, madness and the delusions of madmen represent central and deeply rooted cultural ideas and meanings. Their influence on how we understand delusional thinking, and equally on how it is experienced by its sufferers, seems undeniable and likely to be profound.

Is the category of delusion inescapably linked to the values and associations identified here? Perhaps not. Nonetheless, we employ the concept today pre-theoretically; it is "folk psychology," as philosophers like to say. As such, it seems to be inseparably linked to the distorting cultural meanings within which it has been understood for so long.

Two

Clinical delusions have been grouped in any number of ways. Many pre-twentieth-century inventories focus on what they are delusions about (their "content"). Lycanthropy was the notion that one had turned into a wolf, for example; other delusions involved ideas about jealousy, grandeur, guilt or hypochondriacal matters, and often, the self. More recent taxonomies sort according to structural features, i.e. aspects of the status of delusional content (as untrue, implausible or impossible), and to the tenacity with which delusions are held in the face of countervailing evidence. Clinical delusions have been shown to correspond to these traits only incompletely, however. Some delusions are untrue or implausible – but some are not, and many do not lend themselves to such assessment. Moreover delusions are adhered to with varying degrees of conviction, depending on their content, and also on the stage of their development. (The process of recovery from delusions, for example, seems to include a "double-awareness" phase, when patients are able to question the validity of their delusional beliefs although they have not abandoned them entirely.)[1]

The inventory provided in this chapter is not systematic or comprehensive. Its aim is merely to show dimensions other than the structural ones just noted by which delusions vary.

These include untoward ways they have been acquired; their degree of congruence with the patient's other beliefs, actions, moods and attitudes; the relative complexity of the themes involved; their duration – as fleeting thoughts, long-lived, enduring convictions, or recurrent and episodic belief states; and, finally, their apparent origin, as endogenous, or the result of social contact. Although not the only additional features of delusions identified in clinical lore, these will serve the purpose of demonstrating the further patterns of similarity and difference between different kinds of clinical delusion. They will show that whether or not delusions share some source in brain dysfunction or disorder, as clinical phenomena they seem to be a heterogeneous collection, joined not by shared essential traits so much as by shared social norms about alleviating suffering and dysfunction, averting harm, and rationality. And even a partial inventory of the kinds of delusion encountered in the clinic can establish that case.

As well as being selective, our inventory is arguably incomplete in a second respect (in common with most contemporary discussions). Delusions are identified a-temporally here, as the product or outcome of certain processes not themselves fully described. Yet some, including Jaspers, have approached delusions as psychic processes, whose outcome in belief can only be understood in terms of its cognitive and phenomenological antecedents.[2] The a-temporal approach has some advantages. For instance, it minimizes contested medical and theoretical commitments such as those embodied in the diagnostic category of schizophrenic disorder, and in the model whereby delusions are symptoms of an underlying disease process. Nonetheless, the following descriptions may be too static, running the risk they distort the psychopathology depicted.

DELUSIONAL PARANOID SYSTEMS

The term "paranoid" is misleadingly overused in psychiatry. Sometimes it refers to (and is distinguished by) the particular, wary, suspicious and accusatory content of a type of delusions, and at other times it points to more general characteristics that mark a belief system. (Moreover, the term "paranoid" within psychiatry has been mired in disagreements around the categories of pure paranoia and paraphrenia.[3]) The components of "paranoid" delusional systems in this second, broader sense are our present focus. Regardless of the particular content involved, these are described as extensive and expanding webs of interrelated beliefs – developed by seemingly impeccable inferential reasoning, and involving long-held convictions or attitudes that are maintained, adjusted and adapted in light of (some) new experience. Emil Kraepelin, the nineteenth-century German classifier whose work present-day categories still recognizably follow, speaks of such conditions as leaving the patient with "perfect preservation of clear and orderly thinking, willing and action," and reasoning that is "permanently sensible, clear and reasonable"(Kraepelin 1920: 212–13, 215).

Memoirs of patients sometimes reveal such delusional systems. The great classics in this literature include the *Autobiography of a Schizophrenic Girl* (1951) edited and published by a therapist, Margeurite Sechehaye, and authored by her patient, "Renee." Renee writes that, very soon,

> ". . . I understood that my fear was a cover for guilt, a guilt infinite and awful. . . ."

She then describes daydreams and fantasies, in which

> I had constructed an electric machine to blow up the earth and everyone with it . . . the machine would rob all men of

their brains, thus creating robots obedient to my will alone
. . .

Later, she goes on

. . . I no longer felt guilty about my fantasies, nor did the
guilt have an actual object. It was too pervasive, too
enormous, to be founded on anything definite, and it
demanded punishment. The punishment was indeed horrible,
sadistic – it consisted, fittingly enough, in being guilty. . . . I
felt more and more guilty, immeasurably guilty. Constantly,
I sought to discover what was punishing me so dreadfully,
which was making me so guilty . . .

One day I wrote a letter of entreaty to the unknown author
of my suffering, to the Persecutor, asking him to tell me what
evil I had done, that I might finally know. But because I did not
know where to send my letter, I tore it up.

Some time after, I discovered that the Persecutor was
none other than the electric machine . . . A formidable
interdependence bound all men under the scourge of
culpability. . . . But only some were aware of being part.

(Sechehaye 1994: 47–8)

These strange ideas were interlinked in an all-encompassing
scheme, and Renee describes the way her other responses,
attitudes and actions comported with it. When, later, the
System instructed her to inflict harm on herself, for example,
she obeyed – and felt the justice of such "deserved"
punishment.

MONOTHEMATIC DELUSIONS FROM DEFICIT SYNDROMES

In notable contrast to delusions integrated within such paranoid systems are the single, often bizarre ideas associated

with particular deficit syndromes. Examples include the Capgras patient's conviction that one of her intimates has been replaced by an impostor; Cotard's delusion (the thought that "I am dead"); delusions of unilateral neglect, where patients "disown" a body part ("that is not my leg"), or where the seemingly undeniable fact of some other disability, such as blindness, is denied, as in anosognosia, or Anton's syndrome. These are so-called monothematic delusions, not elaborated, and specific to one simple and limited idea that it is not, or is incompletely, integrated into the rest of the patient's beliefs, feelings and actions. (Intermediate cases will occur that fall readily into neither of the two categories introduced thus far, needless to say.)

Terminological inconsistency and confusion attend this group. As well as "delusions," Cotard's, Capgras and other such conditions have been described as syndromes, deficits and disorders, and also, as we shall see below, as "confabulation," when the latter phenomenon is placed in contrast to delusions proper. Even without a complete characterization of the rather simple ideas and notions making up monothematic states, however, it is apparent that they often lack the very trait most typical of paranoid delusional systems: they are unsystematic. The belief or beliefs are notably disconnected, both from the patient's other mental states and affective responses, and from her behavior. The Capgras patient who claims her husband has been replaced by an impostor is strangely indifferent on the matter of where, if this is not he, her loved one might now be, and why this monstrous change should have occurred. This characteristic mood incongruence has been captured in the expression "fatuous equanimity" – the serene faith of some patients, even in the face of others' evident concern and disbelief, that their beliefs are untroubling and true.[4] Unlike the attitudes of those enter-taining delusional systems, then, fatuous equanimity or some other mismatch between the patient's delusional thought and her other beliefs and responses is often, although as we shall now see, not always, a mark of the monothematic delusions encountered by the neurologist.

In his 1984 memoir of the neurological sequelae of a broken leg, Oliver Sacks provides a compelling first-person account of the phenomenology (as well as the neuro-physiology) of his own experience with Anton's syndrome, or anosognosia. These experiences occurred in a hospital some time after his accident, when the break was healing, and the limb in plaster. The disconcerting and alarming aspects of losing the sense of the injured leg as his own are stressed. There is no equanimity here, fatuous or otherwise – and there are not, at first, convictions of any kind. Sacks is less con-vinced of anything than uncertain and uneasy.

He describes his confusion, seeing the "disowned" plas-tered limb:

> I had felt the leg in front of me . . . but now I could see it wasn't there at all but had got shifted and rotated. . . . I had a sudden sense of mismatch, of profound incongruity – between what I imagined I felt and what I actually saw, between what I had "thought" and what I now found. I felt, for a dizzying, vertiginous moment, that I have been profoundly deceived. . . .

The experience of touching the leg was "inconceivably shocking and uncanny":

> I seemed to have lost "my leg" – which was absurd, for there it was, inside the case, safe and sound – a "fact." How could there be any doubt in the matter? And yet there was. On this

very matter of "having" or "possessing" a leg, I was profoundly doubtful, fundamentally unsure.

This alarming state of uncertainty later resolves itself into what seems closer to a fully delusional state:

> [the leg] became a foreign, inconceivable thing, which I looked at, and touched, without any sense whatever of recognition or relation. It was only then that I gazed at it, and felt I don't know you, you're not part of me, and, further, I don't know this "thing," it's not part of anything. *I had lost my leg*. Again and again I came back to these five words: words which expressed *a central truth* for me, however preposterous they might sound to anyone else. In some sense, then, I had lost my leg. It had vanished; it had gone; it had been cut off at the top. I was now an amputee.
>
> (Sacks 1984: 45,49, 49–50, emphasis added)

Sacks was a neurologist, acutely sensitive to and intrigued by the way his brain and senses were betraying him, and hesitant to draw conclusions about how things were from how they seemed to him. By contrast Babinski, who named this odd syndrome "anosognosia," found no such hesitation in his patients. He describes cases similar to Sacks's own, when the patient's inability to recognize one side of his body led him, comically, to ask the nurse clearing away the breakfast, "Oh, and that arm there – take it away with the tray!" or, in another case, to turn to someone sitting next to him on a train and say "Pardon me, Monsieur, you have your hand on my knee," in reference to his own hand. (Both quotations are from Sacks 1984: 53.)

These contrary responses (of Sacks himself, and those he reports) seem to invite caution in attempting generalizations about the epistemic features of even a single neurological syndrome. All the more reason, it would seem, why we must hesitate before drawing conclusions about the category of clinical delusions *tout court*.

CONFABULATIONS

Seemingly related to simple, monothematic delusions are the "confabulation" syndromes that result from neurological damage. These include the anosognosias described above where the patient denies that he is paralysed, as well as misidentification syndromes such as Capgras, and Korsakoff's syndrome, where memory lapses are patched over with evident falsehoods. Typically, these palpably false beliefs last but a few days and then are gone. They differ markedly in this respect both from many other kinds of clinical delusion, known for their entrenched and persisting quality, and from many more ordinary beliefs and belief states.

The process of confabulation reminds us of more everyday motivated irrationalities – rationalizations and self-deception, for example. Yet it is distinguished from such processes in clinical accounts, and from both lying and pretending. The patient who confabulates seems to be somehow prevented from knowing that his ill-grounded thoughts are ill-grounded.[5] A common occurrence for the few days after stroke has damaged part of the brain is the denial of anosognosia. Something close to fatuous equanimity is demonstrated by a stroke victim who is paralysed on one side. Asked how she feels, she says she is fine, and affirms that both arms are equally strong. Then the doctor requests that she touch her nose with her right hand. She

> . . . pauses a moment, rubs her left shoulder, and offers a confabulation [which she gives with every evidence of sincerely believing it]: "Oh, I've got severe arthritis in my shoulder. It hurts too much to do that."[6]

Confabulation has been correlated with damage to specific areas of the brain. (Particularly implicated with these deficits is damage to the frontal lobes and the corpus callosum.) It has been speculated that the abilities to first construct responses, and then verify the truth or plausibility of those responses, must reflect independent functional systems. Confabulatory patients retain the first ability, even when brain damage has compromised the second.[7]

Terminological confusion abounds here, it will be apparent. (In the clinical literature, the denial of blindness is variously described as Anton's syndrome, a monothematic delusion, and as confabulation, for example.) But as this confusion indicates, the confabulatory process resembles the process of some delusion formation, and the erroneous idea that results (the patient's thought that her arthritis prevents her from moving her right arm, in the example above), might loosely be included in the class of delusions. At the least, confabulation is closely akin to some clinical delusions.

Whether understood as monothematic delusions or as confabulations, the cognitive states associated with these same particular brain deficits and damage have been the source of considerable research attention in recent years. In contrast to most clinical delusions, they either are, or can be plausibly hypothesized to be correlated with neurological deficiencies. The attention they have received, however, stands in contrast to the relative neglect of more common, complex ("polythematic") delusions and particularly to the relationship between these seemingly very different kinds of phenomena. To see this we must again turn to the clinical literature of psychiatry rather than that of neurology. Delusions arise in conditions such as schizophrenia, delusional, and mood disorders. Here, although many have been hypothesized, no correlation with particular defects or deficiencies has yet been established.

"PERCEPTUAL DELUSIONS" AND DELUSIONAL PERCEPTION

Some thought or belief will accompany perceptual experience, whether or not that experience accurately represents the world. But the thought that accompanies naively experienced hallucination may be supposed a kind of delusion. To avoid confusion with delusional perceptions (described presently), we can speak of these mistaken beliefs resulting from the sensory or phenomenal experience of hallucinations – the seeming sounds, sights, smells or touch sensations involved – as perceptual delusions.

The Bavarian painter Christoph Haizmann left a diary (written during 1677–8) recounting experiences that we would today recognize to have been visual, auditory, tactile and even olfactory hallucinations (although he understood them otherwise). Describing one of a series of attacks by demonic forces, he says

> On 26th December I went in the afternoon to Stephen's Cathedral to worship . . . In the evening I went to my bedroom to say my prayers and . . . there was a clap of thunder and a bright flame came down on me so that I again fell into a swoon.
>
> Thereupon my sister came and with her a gentleman who called me by my name, and with that I came to myself. Then it seemed to me as if I were lying in nothing but fire and stench, and could not stand on my feet. I rolled out of my chamber into the room, and rolled around the room until the blood gushed out of my mouth and nose. Then my sister . . . sent for the priests. After they had come the stench and heat disappeared. . . .

On 26th day of December and on 30th December, two evil spirits tortured me with ropes, *which I felt on my limbs* for two days afterwards. They said the torture would be repeated every day until I joined the hermit Order.

(Haizmann 1982: 24, emphasis added)

Haizmann's "it seemed to me" may suggest that the fire and stench he experienced were recognized to be merely fire-like and stench-like, and not taken for real experiences, although he certainly had no doubt, then or later, that these were the effects of demonic influence. But the feel of the ropes, and the subsequent pain they caused, seem to have been experienced as real, and to have wrought a kind of perceptual delusion about them.

Such beliefs force us to reconsider the loose category of delusion on which we have thus far relied. On first encountering (hallucinated) voices, the naive patient assumes the sound came, not from the internal, but from the external world – through his ears. The sophisticated patient who has learnt to doubt the evidence of his senses will unwittingly form a thought as the result of such experience, also. But his thought will be reasonable and appropriate rather than delusory – not "There is a deep voice in this room describing what I do" but "It sounds as if someone is describing what I do" or even "I am having another auditory hallucination."[8]

Ideas that result from faulty perceptual experience are not unwarranted – they are often reasonable inferences. Arguably, then, they are better seen as illusions than delusions. The terminological decision (to call them illusions) may rest, finally, on how delusions are understood, however. For, as we'll see in the next chapter, some theorists have supposed all delusions to represent reasonable inferences from abnormal phenomenal experience, and others that all delusions are themselves a form of hallucination. My own view is that "perceptual delusions" do not rank as delusional states. Delusions are best understood, as they have long been, in terms of the faulty way they are acquired and maintained, rather than merely in terms of their status as false or implausible. As reasonable inferences from misleading perceptual experiences, "perceptual delusions" are not epistemic lapses of the sort by which delusional states are identified.

In contrast to states resulting from hallucination are what are known as "delusional perceptions" or "delusional percepts." These occur when some idea or train of ideas, accompanied by a sense of significance and meaning, is abruptly and unaccountably triggered by everyday, unexceptional, perceptual experiences. These sequences of delusion formation apparently vary greatly, both in their affective tone and in the relative specificity of the sudden ideas that form as a result. Some produce not so much particular thoughts as something closer to a mood: a vague sense of something, as Jaspers puts it, eerie, horrifying, peculiar or remarkable, mystifying or transcendental. When they produce more specific ideas, those ideas are crystal clear, and crisply identified (Jaspers 1997: Vol. 1, 99–100).

These vaguer and sharper kinds of delusional perception need to be considered together as well as separately. In common between them is an immediacy analogous not so much to normal perceptual experience as to the abrupt flashes of insight that bring intuitions and intuitive knowledge. (The German *Wahneinfall* that names these kinds of delusion is most aptly translated "delusional intuition."[9]) Occurring without preamble, they lack any identifiable inferential grounding, or any that makes sense. Psychologists today regard analogous intuitive experiences ("insight" experiences) as related to creative thought, and have isolated the activity in the prefrontal cortex that seems to account for them. (Interestingly, one study of those with less severe forms of disorder [schizotypy] demonstrated enhanced functioning in the creativity and associative thinking demanded for such intuition.[10])

Delusional perceptions are characterized as convictions accompanied by a strong sense of certainty, and this feature also has parallels in other non-clinical states. Of the certainty accompanying the intuitions acquired through religious experience, William James remarks that such intuitions must almost inevitably be regarded as true by their subject; they must be taken to be a kind of reality "which no adverse argument, however unanswerable by you in words, can expel from your belief" (James 1961: 73). When there are no grounds or reasons for holding a belief, James recognizes, there can be no means to evaluate its status as reasonable or warranted, allowing the immediacy and force of the experience to go unchallenged, and unchecked. (We return to these parallels between delusional perception and religious experience in Chapter 6.)

With delusional perceptions of the vaguer kind, Jaspers says, "Something must be going on; the world is changing, a new era is starting. Lights are bewitched and will not burn; something is behind it . . . people are mixed up, they are imposters all, they all look unnatural . . . The streets look suspicious . . ." (Vol. 1, 100). This sort of delusional atmosphere (also often referred to as delusional mood) is depicted by Norma MacDonald, writing of her experience with disorder in the 1950s. She speaks of an "exaggerated state of awareness" in which she lived before, during and after her acute illness:

At first it was as if parts of my brain "awoke" which had been dormant, and I became interested in a wide assortment of people, events, places and ideas which normally would make no impression on me. Not knowing that I was ill, I made no attempt to understand what was happening, but felt that there was some overwhelming significance in all this, produced either by God or Satan, and I felt that I was duty-bound to ponder on each of these new interests, and the more I pondered the worse it became. The walk of a stranger on the street could be a "sign" to me which I must interpret. Every face in the windows of a passing streetcar would be engraved on my mind, all of them concentrating on me and trying to pass me some sort of message . . . By the time I was admitted to hospital I had reached a stage of "wakefulness" when the brilliance of light on a window sill or the colour of blue in the sky would be so important it could make me cry . . . Completely unrelated events became intricately connected in my mind.

(MacDonald 1960: 220–1)

Odd, vague and mood-like, atmospheric experiences such as these can be placed in contrast to the sharper, clearer delusional perceptions, yet Jaspers emphasized that both kinds of state share a seemingly non-inferential quality. When a simple perceptual experience (the sight of faces in the windows in passing streetcars) unaccountably contained signs for MacDonald, they came without intermediaries, and with the suddenness of non-inferential insight.

The above passage also illustrates the way the global and all-encompassing aspect of these delusions is interwoven with that quality of immediate, intuitive apprehension. MacDonald's state of "wakefulness," when even the walk of a stranger on the street contained meaning, was part of a mood-like apprehension of the world around her. Moods are distinguished from other feelings in being over or about no particular thing. The delusional atmosphere pervades every aspect of MacDonald's experience, making the object of the experience an expansive one – it is everything apprehended.

Moods are a normal part of psychic life, indeed, some have insisted that they are ever present, and a foundational aspect of human consciousness.[11] But they normally match the thoughts accompanying them (as MacDonald's ideas were congruent with her state of exalted alertness). It is thus not incongruence that accounts for the unreasonable quality of MacDonald's state but its inferential status.[12] The brilliance of the light on the window sill does not provide a reason for anticipating something grand and important.

Delusional perceptions of a more precise kind are illustrated employing a famous case introduced by Jaspers. The sight of the marble table tops in a café prompted not a vague sense of doom, in one patient, but the precise conviction that the world was coming to an end.[13]

RECURRENT DELUSIONS

Mood disorders also regularly reach the status of psychosis and give rise to delusional thinking. According to one estimate, for example, no less than 58 percent of manic patients and 15 percent of those who are depressed have psychotic symptoms.[14] Classificatory tangles are involved here, for today's findings challenge the strict Kraepelinian division between schizophrenia (*dementia praecox*) and manic-depressive conditions.[15] However, these need not concern us. The delusions associated with mania and depression are mood-congruent, matching the feelings accompanying them (for this reason they are not categorized as delusions proper by Jaspers). They also have another feature that distinguishes them from the kinds of delusion identified thus far. They are sometimes recurrent, fading and returning with the changes of the often bipolar conditions involved.[16] The mood congruent feature of such conditions, if not this distinctive pattern of recurrence, is readily illustrated by John Custance's description of the elation that formed the background, as he says, to his experience of the whole manic state:

> It seems to me that all my wishes are coming true, that all my ambitions, in work, and in play, political, financial, personal, are going to be realized, that vital secrets of the Universe are being revealed to me and so on. This applies not only to normal wishes and ambitions but to *wholly abnormal* and unreasonable ones. . . . All nature and life, all spirits, are co-operating and connected with me; all things are possible.
>
> (Custance 1952: 51, emphasis added)

Whether all Custance's mood-congruent states would rank as delusional may be doubted. But his "wholly abnormal and unreasonable" wishes and ambitions seemingly do. And to the extent that these same ideas returned with the return of subsequent manic episodes he describes in his long memoir, we must recognize in reoccurring delusions another dimension along which delusions exhibit variation (Although even less frequently acknowledged in recent work on delusions, cycloid [or periodic] psychoses exhibit a similar profile; they have been described as combining schizophrenic symptoms with a manic-depressive course [Fish 1964].[17])

FOLIES À DEUX AND GROUP DELUSIONS

In folie à deux or shared delusional disorder one person persuades an intimate of his own delusional ideas.[18] The following case history from a recent discussion of folie à deux describes the way a mother (a fifty-five-year-old widow) influenced her adult son with delusional parasitosis. First, her own delusions formed:

> . . . she suddenly noticed that many dandruff flakes fell from her neck, which turned out to be bugs when she examined them closely. Then, she noticed that many bugs were attached to the ceiling, were flying, got stuck on her arms or legs . . . The bugs laid eggs in her skin and were bothering her a lot when the eggs in her skin suddenly bounced up at once when male bugs sprayed semen onto her body. The symptoms continued despite her efforts . . . spraying her house and her body with pesticides and wiping off her skin after spreading oil onto her body. The symptoms did not improve even after dermatologic treatment. . . .

Unable to find work, the son moved in with his mother:

> Shortly after moving, he noticed that lots of dandruff fell on the blanket. When he and his mother took a close look, they noticed that the dandruffs were moth larvae. He felt itchy . . . bought mothballs and placed them in several places in the house. . . . The bugs flew and got stuck in his arms or legs, flying bugs suddenly burst into powder, which got into his nose and mouth . . . He could not even sleep because it was so itchy and painful. [Further efforts to get rid of the bugs using pesticides failed.] . . . Only the patient and his mother could see the bugs. . . .

Eventually, because of the believed infestation of their house, the pair moved to a series of motel accommodations.[19]

We return to cases such as this one in Chapter 5. *Folies à deux* are of interest in falling midway between individualistic delusions apparently arising from within the brain and psyche of the patient herself, and delusional ideas transferred through other people. By the twenty-first century, the individualistic emphasis of psychiatric and psychological theorizing, including the presumption that severe disorder is "endogenous," and cannot arise from factors external to the person, has mostly severed the study of clinical delusions as they are normally understood from the delusional thinking apparently brought about by contact with others who are not intimates. Yet mistaken and sometimes dangerous ideas and belief states are transferred through the social context. They are seen in the clinic because they can result in self-destructive syndromes. And many of the effects of other people in bringing about delusional states such as these seem indistinguishable within the miscellany of cases introduced thus far. The beliefs about body image and the world that lead to pathologies like cutting, bulimia, anorexia and suicidal behavior, seem to be as implausible, ill-grounded and tenaciously maintained as many other clinical delusions. However, these conditions are not only wanting or irrational because of their behavioral effects and their often palpably inaccurate or implausible content (such as the emaciated anorexic woman's conviction that she is fat). Sometimes, at least, they are not acquired through ordinary social learning but are instead "caught," like a contagious disease. In failing to conform to rationality norms governing how beliefs are acquired, they may be seen to resemble the "delusional perceptions" that, without preliminaries, impose groundless convictions imbued with meaning and significance.

The appropriateness of the term "delusion" here is provided with a fuller defense in a later chapter, when some of the long and puzzling history of "group" delusions is told. Group delusions fit among the conditions we have looked at thus far not only because they share several features in common, but also because they are associated with behavioral epidemics of self-destructiveness. Transgressing other mental health norms about social functioning, they appear in the clinic.

PATCHWORK

Even setting aside the intermediate and less clear-cut cases – the "delusion-like" and "overvalued" ideas making up the penumbra around many, if not all, clinical delusions – the miscellany recognized as clinical delusions still forms a complex pattern. A handful of different features or dimensions were identified at the start of this chapter: the seemingly irrational way these delusions have been acquired, their congruence with the patient's other mental states and behavior, the relative simplicity or complexity of the themes involved, their duration (fleeting, long-lived or reoccurring), and their apparently endogenous or social origins. Exploring delusions with respect to these features, we discover a patchwork of similarities and differences. Paranoid systems involve multiple, interlinked beliefs often marked by their internal logic and their enduring course; they may be acquired through unexceptional, if ambiguous, perceptual experience; they are often integrated into the patient's other mental states and behavior, and they, typically, are complex. The monothematic delusions and confabulations associated with disease and damage to the brain, are of brief, sometimes even fleeting, duration, and involve simple themes detached, in many cases, from the rest of the patient's psychic life and behavior. Some perceptual delusions involve precise ideas and themes, others not; both kinds (vague and precise) are acquired in ways that contravene epistemic norms. The mood-congruent delusions of mania, depression and bipolar disorder are often integrated into the patient's life and behavior, but they fade and recur according to the course of these recurrent conditions. *Folies à deux*, although they usually involve implausible ideas, often tenaciously adhered to, are seemingly acquired – for the second partner, at least – unexceptionally. Group delusions, in contrast, are sometimes acquired by a process of social contagion which is contrary to epistemic norms.

OVERVALUED IDEAS AND DELUSION-LIKE IDEAS

Clinical writing suggests the ubiquity of gray-area, quasi-delusional states: ideas that more closely resemble the implausible and yet sometimes firmly held convictions and preoccupations of ordinary life. First-person accounts confirm these observations again and again, sometimes even recognizing the gradations involved. Bleuler quotes a description from Forel's patient, "Miss L.S.":

> . . . half driven by an inspiration, half-aware and half-willing, I created for myself a role which I carried on playing and reciting. I became so enwrapped in, so completely absorbed by, this role that I acted in accordance with it, *without* precisely believing that I was identical with the persons portrayed. Sure enough in all this, there were many gradations from the borderline of the delusional idea,

perhaps from the delusion itself, to the merely exuberant or
excited mood.

(Bleuler 1950: 128, emphasis added)

Do these ideas reach the level of real, clinical delusions? The
answer seems to be: not quite, but close, as Miss L.S. takes
pains to point out.

What are known as overvalued ideas represent one sort of
quasi-delusional, or delusion-like, state of this kind.[20] The term
"overvalued idea" (Wernicke 1900) has come to mean an isolated but otherwise unexceptional preoccupation of such emotional importance to the individual that it is maintained tenaciously, and affects identity and motivation. (So embedded,
overvalued ideas are predictably resistant to treatment.)

Clinical descriptions of overvalued ideas suggest they differ
little, except in degree, from more everyday convictions –
especially perhaps, those involving moral, ideological, metaphysical and religious themes. Overvalued ideas are said to be
held "too strongly" and to preoccupy the individual's mental
life "too much."[21] Some obvious problems accompany all
solely normative categories such as these (how strong, and
how much, is too strong and too much?). But even setting
these aside, this account seems vulnerable to examples about
saints, heroes and reformers from everyday life, whose preoccupations frequently exceed such statistical norms, and
some of whom we may be reluctant to judge even mildly
disordered.

Overvalued ideas are said to differ from obsessional and
phobic ones in feeling natural rather than intrusive, and being
acquiesced to without resistance, rather than regarded as
senseless or futile.[22] When it comes to separating overvalued
ideas from delusions proper, however, the clinical literature is
less helpful. In contrast to delusions proper, overvalued ideas

develop comprehensibly out of a given personality and situation, according to Jaspers. But typical overvalued ideas include those of hypochondria (the patient becomes over-concerned with health and convinced he is seriously ill); dismorphophobia (when the idea is about some insufficiency of bodily appearance), and the parasitophobic conviction that one is infested. In addition, are the preoccupations known as the querulous paranoid states (the person persistently seeks legal remedy after some occurrence that seems too trivial to warrant doing so), and attitudes of abnormal sexual jealousy. Categories such as these will not serve to distinguish frankly delusional beliefs about these ideas over bodily health, appearance, imagined infestation, injustice and infidelity, any more than they will strongly held normal preoccupations over those same matters.

Either overvalued ideas are milder forms of delusion or delusion-like ideas. Or, if they are not, we are left with little to distinguish overvalued ideas from the staunchly held convictions of everyday life.

Jaspers would deny that many of the states described in this chapter are any more than delusion-like phenomena – distinguishable in degree but also kind from delusions properly so called, which he speaks of as "the vague crystallizations of blurred delusional experiences and diffuse, perplexing self-references which cannot be sufficiently understood in terms of the personality or the situation," and must instead be understood as "symptoms of a disease process" (Jaspers 1997: Vol. 1, 107). But whether delusions may or may not be understood is too complex and too controversial an issue for this definition to be sufficient, as we'll see in Chapter 4.

Three

A thorough review of the burgeoning contemporary research on delusions by philosophers, cognitive psychologists, and brain scientists will not be embarked on here. But three intersecting controversies over clinical delusions, each the focus of important research, will introduce the kind – and serve to illustrate the extent – of conceptual uncertainties surrounding clinical delusions. First, researchers divide between those putting forward a continuum model and those attempting to establish – or assuming – that a categorical difference distinguishes clinical ("psychotic," "true" or "primary") delusions. Next, although traditional accounts depict delusions as belief states, and certainly the qualities customarily ascribed to delusions are the attributes of belief states, this "doxastic" analysis (delusions are beliefs) is controversial in a number of ways. Some propose delusions be described in equally familiar but different terms, while for others they are *sui generis*, falling within none of the familiar categories used to distinguish mental faculties and states. And thirdly, there is no consensus over the kind of explanation required for clinical delusions. Recent accounts depict them as a product of flawed reasoning, as normal responses to abnormal, inexplicable or disconcerting experiences – and as some combination of both of these.

CONTINUUM VERSUS CATEGORICAL ACCOUNTS

The similarities between clinical delusions and common forms of irrationality and illusion have impressed one collection of researchers, while others have seen, and stressed, the differences.

If delusional thinking in some ways resembles normal errors of judgement, then a difference of more than magnitude and disabling consequences would most resoundingly ensure their status as separate in kind. That difference, the categorical view anticipates, likely lies with deficiencies in the brain or cognitive processing. The delusional person's errors reflect some dysfunction or incapacity which he cannot, or cannot easily, overcome. The specific deficiencies associated with neurological disorders are particularly revealing here, and doubly so. Due to disease or damage to the brain, for example, some part of the commonplace ability of facial recognition is sometimes lost, and results in bizarre misidentification delusions like that of the Capgras patient convinced her husband has been replaced by an impostor. The Capgras patient's recognition of the familiar face has become disengaged from the positive affective response that would usually accompany it as the result of a right hemisphere lesion, it has been explained, so that the perceived person is said to "look right, but feel wrong."[1] From this we learn the area in the brain where such functioning takes place but also, more generally, how sub-capacities indissolubly fused in normal experience come apart into separate functional units.

Intricate, ingenious and complex evidence supports these incompatible conclusions about whether delusions rest on a continuum or are distinct kinds. Yet the facts on each side, while persuasive, are less than conclusive. In particular, two sets of observations (both introduced earlier), have been taken to constitute reasons supporting the continuum position: the clinical states apparently lying in the penumbra between psychotic and more normal states (delusion-like ideas, delusion-like notions, and overvalued ideas); and, even among clinical delusions proper, the sheer variety to be found. Neither observation taken alone, nor their combination, is entirely dispositive, however, in establishing whether clinical delusions are categorically different from more normal cognitive states.

Challenges to the continuum view point to the preliminary ("pre-theoretical") nature of any observations about clinical delusions: such an immature science cannot be expected to have ascertained *what* distinguishes the category of delusions, it is held.

Nonetheless, the burden of proof is unevenly distributed between those asserting continuum and those asserting categorical positions. Those emphasizing the continuum hold the high ground, and the burden lies with those who would unseat their analysis. This is for moral and social considerations, however, not methodological ones. Merely pointing to the commonalities between clinical delusions, delusion-like ideas, and everyday states of irrational conviction is not enough, methodologically, to resolve the matter. According to the models of psychiatric disorder often adhered to by those favoring a categorical approach, for example, delusions occur as the symptoms of underlying disease processes. As such, their differences in disabling severity will be no more difficult to explain than the degrees by which fever occurs as the sign of various bodily ailments. It is true that the applicability of the categorical disease model to psychiatric disorder has been questioned.[2] But even without it, other medical analogies permit recognition of a continuum of disease-caused symptoms shading into normal states. (The way blood pressure levels shade from the pathological to the normal range is an example.) As long as such analogies and presuppositions are granted, the categorical analysis can be maintained, even in the face of apparent shading between normal and clinical states.

Arguably, the evidence from the variety of clinical delusions does somewhat better in supporting the continuum approach. If delusions are analogous to the raised temperature in ordinary medicine, then even the fact that no single underlying disease process may be responsible for them would not defeat the categorical model. Raised temperature is a symptom common to any number of different diseases; so too, delusions perhaps result from many quite distinct underlying processes. These may reflect the standard categories (schizophrenia, mood disorders, and so on) in the way that much contemporary biomedical psychiatry implies. Alternatively, they may correspond to the new faculty psychology of cognitive neuroscience: separate functionally defined processes that have not thus far shown themselves to correspond to orthodox diagnostic categories.

All that said, the "patchwork" sketched in Chapter 2 seems to belie the idea that delusions are one category, or one thing in the world, nonetheless. Rather than comprising a central core surrounded by a penumbra of gray-area cases, clinical delusions vary one from another in a complex miscellany. Moreover, research on different delusions has implicated causal antecedents within an assortment of apparently unrelated brain locations and systems.

As "practical" kinds, the distressing, disabling and sometimes dangerous states making up clinical delusions form a category of sorts, and it is one with significant real-world moral, practical and policy implications. But it is not the sort of category the adherents of the categorical model had in mind, i.e. one which constitutes a kind in nature the way that, say, molecules and quarks do.[3]

The philosophical category of "natural kind" is a contested one itself, its diverse and warring definitions determining how many sorts of thing in the world are elected to stand beside the likes of molecules and quarks. According to the fairly accommodating model Richard Samuels adopts, delusions may comprise one or several natural kinds.[4] Yet for that, he recognizes, some unifying element would need to be present. Natural kinds are individuated by their causal essences, as he puts it. Only if the many different subtypes of mechanism responsible for delusions are themselves *of the same kind*, will delusions constitute a natural kind like molecules and quarks.[5] Although he can sketch what this sort of unity would look like (called for would be a mechanism that explained all delusions without merely deferring to the fact that they produce similar effects), Samuels admits that the question of whether delusions possess such unity remains unanswered. The options are all still on the table, then: a causal essence may be uncovered, proving that all true delusions indeed belong to a single, overarching (natural kind) category; we may settle for a group of categories (persecutory delusions one kind, perhaps, delusions of grandeur another, and so on); or there may be nothing more than a complex, multidimensional miscellany of non-natural, practical kinds.

The promise of each of the first two hypotheses has been taken to warrant vigorous exploratory research. (And arguably the presence of exemplars in for instance, persecutory delusions, delusions of grandeur, *et cetera*, may be sufficient to guide explanatory efforts.[6]) But disagreements between these two groups of theorists remain over whether continuum or categorical models are more apt for delusions.

Also implicated here are definitional questions: what might count as an adequate definition of all, or particular kinds of, delusions, and whether an essentialist definition is possible – or necessary? How and whether to define delusions may have to await further research on the issues outlined above.[7] Earlier definitions purporting to cover all delusions have now been set aside by most researchers. (In the clinical context, other features also contribute to diagnoses, and these rough and ready guides are usually sufficient.) Some theorists hold hope of finding an essentialist definition, naming necessary and sufficient conditions. Others have proposed that since clinical delusions are heterogeneous, we can at best look for a set of criteria some number of which will be sufficient to attribute delusion (Oltmanns 1988; Munro 1999). Settling for this menu (or "nomological") approach is acknowledging that no characteristics may be common to all delusions or even to subsets of them. If so, in a conclusion apparently supported by clinical observation, states will vary in the way, but also the degree, to which they are delusional.

DOXASTIC POSITIONS: DELUSIONS AS BELIEFS

Delusions are belief-like, but are they beliefs? Several positions have been staked out in answer to this question: all delusions are beliefs; none are; some are; the evidence is equivocal.[8]

It has been pointed out that the French *délire* conveys a more encompassing and less solely cognitive meaning than that often accorded to the English "delusion."[9] And delusions may better be understood as ideas, judgements, feelings, thoughts, or imaginings, rather than beliefs, others have proposed – or as hallucinated beliefs that, due to an inability to distinguish her imaginings from her beliefs their subject mistakenly believes she believes. By assigning delusions to the category of judgements, for instance, we accommodate the many delusions that appear to be complex assessments, rather than straightforward beliefs. "Attitude" seems to better fit the cognitive, affective and volitional elements and inferential patterns that give rise to some delusional (or paranoid) systems. The "delusional atmosphere" (over or about the whole of experience but no particular aspect of it), lacks the specificity of belief, and has the affective tone that bespeaks feelings or moods rather than solely cognitive states.[10] As fleeting states, some delusions better resemble ideas, thoughts or notions. And the complex attitude involved in imagining also resembles that taken toward some delusions.[11] (That said, the "meta-cognitive" analysis relegating all delusions to imaginings mistakenly confused with true beliefs has been subject to compelling criticism by Tim Bayne and Elizabeth Pacherie.[12] They show that such attempts conflate different notions of imagining; are implausible in application to several kinds of delusion; and fail to explain why the monitoring of imagining should be deficient in the case of some and not other beliefs, for example.)

In addition, traits associated with ordinary beliefs also seem to be absent from many delusions. Delusions are often ill-grounded, for example: in some, grounds are entirely absent, in others they are apparently recognized by the patient, but disregarded or discounted. The "fatuous equanimity" that seems to separate these ideas from their normal affective accompaniments is an example of another such feature, as is the "behavioral inertia" by which those with delusions fail to act on them. More generally, delusional ideas are sometimes strangely detached from the rest of the subject's other beliefs.

These traits, or some very similar, are found in many contemporary discussions aiming to refute the "doxastic" position. At best a subset of delusions elude these criteria for being beliefs, however. Many delusions (as we have seen) are defended on the basis of elaborate grounds and seemingly held with conviction; delusions are sometimes deeply integrated into the psyche, motivation and character of a person, and acted upon entirely appropriately; elaborate delusional systems often show a remarkable holism, each belief carefully linked to another by impeccable logic.

Ordinary believers are also wanting when it comes to these traits, moreover. Leaping to unwarranted conclusions, maintaining beliefs with insufficient evidence, and exhibiting every imaginable form of behavioral inertia are commonplace in ordinary, non-clinical believers. The conviction that one should embark on some healthful or uplifting practice is notoriously prone to slippage between intention and action. Wishing to act on a belief but being prevented by timidity or prudence is, we recognize, simply human. Undeniably, with the ordinary case of believing one should act and failing to do so, qualification is often introduced ("If you genuinely believed that, you'd do it"), or interference from a weak will is attributed. But we do not customarily use the presence of behavioral inertia to withhold belief status.

The features of belief raised in these discussions seem to reflect ideals rather than descriptions of actual human psychology. It is (statistically) normal to be imperfectly rational. If nothing else, our "finitary predicament" (Bayne and Pacherie 2005) – not enough time or memory – means that we must settle for a lesser rationality. Inevitably we will exhibit some of the want of rationality that has been used by theorists to try to establish that delusional thinking cannot involve beliefs.[13]

Another way to approach whether delusions are beliefs asks if there is a fact of the matter about whether a person believes her delusion.[14] There may be such a fact, yet we may not be able to know it; alternatively, there may be no such fact. Thinking about the first option (there is a fact of the matter but it is unknowable), we confront the relation of mind, language and world, and the status of first-hand reports of any subjective experience, normal or abnormal. It is the patient who must tell us about those delusions, and the patient on the basis of whose assertions each of the claimed features of delusional thinking depend. Yet, if we recollect the discouraging history of introspectionist psychology, it becomes clear that complete trust in this method, whether applied to patients or to ordinary subjects, may be misplaced. The introspectionist program of Titchener foundered on an unknowable "fact" – whether all thoughts included images. When we cannot with full confidence ascertain how, and whether, normal subjects believe, how much less promising seems the prospect of determining whether deluded patients do. Here, then, is the most radical response to controversies over whether delusions are beliefs. Our means of discovering the nature and status of other people's mental states – or even discovering the nature and status of our own, for that matter – are imperfect. Rather than clear facts of the matter here, there seems very often to be indeterminacy.

Since the demise of the introspectionist program, the philosopher's armchair has been the site of much introspectionist study. (As, of course, it had always been.) And many an insight about the mind has been so acquired, undeniably. But consciousness has also been explored, in recent years, by laborious neo-introspectionist methods such as those of Russell Hurlburt.[15] Using normal subjects as well as psychiatric patients, this work employs something close to the approach proposed by Jaspers many years ago: in the course of conversation, the patient's assertions are invoked, clarified and tested. Such programs have permitted the elimination of sources of confusion and error associated with introspection and introspectionism. But the uncertainties, vagueness and conflicting interpretations that have emerged also highlight the several indeterminacies evident in introspective report. Not only whether there can be imageless thought, but the nature of beliefs, emotions, perception, attention and all subjective states still want for definitive accounts derived from introspection. Moreover, these indeterminacies do not merely enter for the observer, although that they must do. They prove themselves inherent in subjective report – no matter how articulate, how analytic, how observant, how careful and fair that subject might be.

Hurlburt and his colleagues speak of the qualifications, shifting descriptions, and explicitly voiced doubts and uncertainties that accompany introspective reports from normal subjects as "subjunctifier" phrases. And the frequency of these doubts about the accuracy of statements – expressed as "I think," "It's like a . . .," "kind of," "that's the best way I can think to describe it" – is one of the most evident aspects of Hurlburt's findings.

Yet none of this can come as a surprise to those who have read first-hand accounts of psychotic experience. Subjective descriptions of both delusions and hallucinations are regularly accompanied by elaborate qualifications that echo these uncertainties over how to capture and represent such experiences. *Autobiography of a Schizophrenic Girl*, introduced earlier, provides innumerable examples. In one passage, the author describes an alarming childhood experience that occurred while jumping rope at recess:

> Two little girls were turning a long rope while two others jumped in from either side to meet and cross over. When it came to my turn and I saw my partner jump toward me where we were to meet and cross over, I was seized with panic; I did not recognize her. Though I saw her as she was, still, it was not she. Standing at the other end of the rope, she had seemed smaller, but the nearer we approached each other, the taller she grew, the more she swelled in size.
>
> I cried out, "Stop Alice, you look like a lion; you frighten me!" At the sound of the fear in my voice which I tried to dissemble under the guise of fooling, the game came to an abrupt halt. The girls looked at me, amazed, and said, "You're silly – Alice, a lion? You don't know what you're talking about."
>
> Then the game began again. Once more my playmate became strangely transformed and, with an excited laugh, once more I cried out, "Stop, Alice, I'm afraid of you; you're a lion!"

At this point in her narrative, the author pauses to further explain the previous remark. Actually, she qualifies:

> . . . I didn't see a lion at all; it was only an attempt to describe the enlarging image of my friend and the fact that I didn't recognize her. . . .
>
>   (These passages are from Sechehaye 1994: 23)

Rather than a hallucination, or a perceptual delusion, this careful re-formulation makes it clear that the experience was so strange it beggared accurate description.

A similar struggle to find words for his unsettling experiences is one of the most prominent features of Daniel Schreber's great work *Memoirs of My Nervous Illness* (1903). Schreber qualifies and rephrases in his attempt to depict the strange ideas and thoughts that assailed him, and the range of doubts and uncertainties he entertained over them. Indeed, it might be said that the memoir has twin epistemological themes, each resulting in an endless series of "subjunctifications." First, Schreber believes the ideas and experiences resist description. As spiritual or mystical matters, they can at best be depicted through metaphor and simile. In addition, however, his own stance as a knower is questioned – his conviction and confidence not only in the accuracy of his description, but in the reality of the experiences themselves.

The first point can be put by saying that most of Schreber's experiences from those years in the asylum are, in his view, ineffable – incapable of being expressed in words. In order to avoid misleading presuppositions based on sense-knowledge, Schreber appealed to the neurology of his time: he speaks of "nerves" in describing how he is affected during these mystical experiences. But his are not the nerves of neurology, for – through the mediation of supernatural "rays" – they are affected metaphysically, or spiritually, not physically. We are used to thinking of all impressions we receive from the outer world as derived from the five senses, he explains in one passage. But

> . . . in the case of a human being who like myself has entered into contact with rays and whose head is in consequence so to speak illuminated by rays, this is not so at all. I receive light and sound sensations which are projected direct on to my inner nervous system by the rays;

for their reception the external organs of seeing and hearing are not necessary.

(Schreber 2000: 121n)

Because of the nature of the experiences, even figurative and metaphorical language must fall short in accounting for the influence of mystical rays: "To make myself at least somewhat comprehensible I shall have to speak much in images and similes, which may at times perhaps be only approximately correct," he says (Schreber 2000: 120–1). Metaphors may be apt or clumsy or misleading. But they cannot be incorrect. Clearly, Schreber wants his assertions *exempted from any simple assessment as to accuracy*.

A deeper uncertainty revealed in the memoir is not about how Schreber is to convey these ideas, but how he actually apprehends them. One of the most elaborated notions he describes is of having been transformed by the rays into a woman (in order to be able to bring forth another human in a depopulated world). Yet, he writes of these ideas as "my so-called delusions"; and the "pictures" he is able to evoke of himself being transformed into a woman, he insists, are only the products of his imagination.

> The object seen can be either visual (eye) impressions, . . . or *images which I can cause at will on my inner nervous system* by imagination, so that they come visible to the rays . . . [these events are] in the soul language called the "picturing" of human beings.

(Schreber 2000: 148)

Of his transformation from male to female, he later remarks that he needed to shave, for "to support *my imagination of being a female* . . . a mustache would naturally have been an insurmountable obstacle for this *illusion*" (Schreber 2000: 181, emphasis added).

Observing Schreber's qualifications and hesitations Louis Sass has attributed to them a quality described as the product of Schreber's own consciousness, rather than enjoying an existence that was "independent or objective" (Sass 1994: 8). As Sass says, Schreber's delusional experiences retain for him "an aura that labels it not as reality but as only an experience" (Sass 1994: 27). Moreover, the tentative, non-literal and self-aware quality of Schreber's assertions is even more apparent in the original German. Translators of the *Memoirs* have omitted many recurring phrases and particles that are deemed awkward and otiose, Sass reminds us, including "in part," "on the other hand," "so to speak," "up to a point," and "in a way."

These features of Schreber's memoir are emblematic of schizophrenic experience and communication for Sass, illustrating the claim, to which we will return in a later chapter, that conditions like Schreber's exhibit a quasi-solipsistic isolation from any intersubjective reality. But more notably, I suggest, they bear a strong similarity to the qualifications Hurlburt found in normal subjects asked to provide introspective accounts of their experience. Rather than distinguishing the experience of schizophrenia, they will likely mark *any careful attempt to recount introspective experience*.

What conclusions can be drawn about the controversy over the doxastic status of delusions? Certainly several of the possibilities laid out at the start of this chapter remain options. Not all delusions, and perhaps not any, can usefully be regarded as hallucinations, or imaginings. Our category of belief may not accommodate all delusional states, true. But nor is that category precise enough, or sufficiently agreed upon, to exclude all delusions from the status of beliefs. (It may be that "belief" conceals different meanings, for example, each with incompatible epistemological implications.[16]) On the other hand, delusions may be a sufficiently natural kind of kind as to be understood as *sui generis*.

ALTERNATIVE CAUSAL ACCOUNTS

Some research attempts to establish flaws in the way delusions are formed and or maintained, epistemic errors which, while they may not be within the subject's control, often resemble and seem to differ only in magnitude from those more commonplace flaws of reasoning and judgement that are. (These have been dubbed "top-down" theories.) Compelling evidence from neuropsychiatry has linked deficits and damage occurring in particular parts or systems of the brain to some delusional states and confabulatory responses; these have generated further ("bottom-up") causal hypotheses identifying the underlying deficit to which the delusion (or confabulation) appears to be a response. Most causal models combine these two explanatory approaches. At least those delusions that are more monothematic and unsystematic, it is argued, result only when both factors occur. (We shall return to these two-factor theories in a moment.)

Hypothesized flaws in the reasoning of those with delusions trace to the 1940s, when laboratory studies exploded the idea that an incapacity of inferential logic distinguished schizophrenic reasoning.[17] More recent efforts seeking to show that other reasoning deficiencies are always present, while somewhat supported by laboratory studies, are also regarded by some as inconclusive.[18] And this inconclusiveness was one factor encouraging Brendan Maher to speculate that the person with delusions may suffer abnormal, anomalous experience, to which the formation of the delusion represented a normal and appropriate response.[19]

Maher's hypothesis was derived from a body of psychological research establishing that in response to anomalous perceptual and hypnotically-induced experiences and other forms of suggestion, normal subjects can readily be driven to adopt implausible ideas. Perhaps the best known of these studies was conducted in the 1960s, when normal subjects were provided with the laboratory task of tracking a target while, on a screen, they watched the progress of what appeared to be their hands holding the joystick. Unbeknownst to one group of these subjects, the hand represented on the screen was not their own, and it subtly failed to comply with the intentions they formed. Asked afterwards to explain their poor performance at the task, these subjects offered a range of seemingly delusion-like responses: "It was done by magic"; "My hand took over and my mind was not able to control it"; "I was hypnotized"; "My hand was controlled by an outside physical force"; "I tried hard to make my hand go to the left, but my hand tried harder and was able to overcome me and went off to the right."[20]

If normal subjects can so easily be prompted to adopt implausible ideas, the only distinguishing feature of those whose delusions are clinically significant might seem that they are formed in response to anomalous sensory or affective experience. "Two-factor" theorists resist this conclusion, however. Anomalous experiences (the odd one known as *déjà vu*, for example) do not always lead to delusions, they point out. The added feature that would convert "It was done by magic" or "My hand was controlled by an outside physical force" from a tentative, passing thought into a delusional conviction, must be found in some additional deficit or failure relating to belief acceptance – something to do with how first-person experience, or stored background knowledge, or the testimony of those around one, is employed in epistemic processing.

The nature of this second factor (the flawed epistemic processing prompted by the hypothesized anomalous experience), remains unclear, and has been characterized in a number of ways. An inability to "reject a candidate for belief on the grounds of its implausibility and its inconsistency with everything else that the patient knows," is one formulation.[21] In normal reasoners such an ability to screen beliefs is (usually) exercised with effortless inattention, yet it is at the core of what we understand to be proper belief formation.

Hypothesized second factors have also been focused on reasoning bias: as they show themselves in the laboratory, for example, inferences are drawn somewhat more rapidly by delusional than by normal subjects, indicating what has come to be called a "jumping to conclusions" bias.[22] And important research in cognitive psychology has focused on biased explanations offered for events and experiences (so-called attribution style), that seem to distinguish those suffering particular delusions. (For example, explanations of untoward events are normally deflected away from oneself and onto external circumstances [this is known as self-serving bias]; those with a paranoid attributional style, in addition, tend to attribute negative events to other people, not to circumstances. [They are said to make "external-personal" attributions rather than "external-situational" ones].)

One analysis postulates that delusions occur when the person's "framework propositions" – unreasoned, unjustifiable, pre-reflexive assumptions that ground our ability to engage in the world – have been lost or become inoperative.[23] Another theory points to the part played by affective states. A group of "existential" feelings, including those of familiarity and unfamiliarity, function as evidence, it is argued; disturbed or inoperative, they interfere with the patient's belief formation.[24]

Hypothesizing deficiencies in delusional patients' understanding of the mental states, beliefs, actions and intentions of those around them (their "theory of mind") represents an account of what the second factor might involve that moves beyond the narrowly individualistic conceptions of these other hypotheses.[25] And once we acknowledge the social nature of belief, other possibilities arise. Reasoning deficits may involve a failure to read others, as the "theory of mind" theory suggests; but more obviously, it might involve a failure to integrate others' communications, or an inability to employ the usual means of intersubjective belief verification.

Much of this two-factor theorizing has been focused on simple monothematic delusions, and even here, researchers admit that puzzles remain – over why such reasoning defects do not affect a fuller range of the patient's beliefs, for example, and why some patients appear to appreciate the implausibility of their delusional beliefs without being able to relinquish them.[26] But in explicitly limiting their attention to monothematic delusions, these two-factor theorists have another task remaining. They must also explain what bearing their two-factor account might have – if any – on other kinds of delusions. Clinical evidence suggests that complex delusions are often triggered by perceptual experience that is at worst ambiguous and open to interpretation, not particularly anomalous or alarmingly inexplicable. So the presumption that an anomalous experience provides part of the explanation of delusion formation is just that – a presumption.

Although not the only source of disagreement over delusions, the three controversies outlined here have dominated much of the scholarly debate in the last decade of the twentieth and the beginning of the twenty-first centuries. Equally controversial, but also evident in earlier research, is the related issue dealt with next: the alleged meaninglessness of the content of delusions.

Four

Assumptions about the intelligibility of delusions pervade the ideas introduced thus far, and this is an additional issue over which researchers are divided. Echoing Jaspers's analysis, some have held clinical delusions (or at least a subset of them) to be without meaning for their possessor, and thus incomprehensible to the observer. Others would find, or attribute, meaning, even in delusions that are seemingly unintelligible.

This difference between denying and attributing meaning to delusional and psychotic thought could hardly be more significant philosophically. Moreover, it is a disagreement of considerable complexity, with its own historical context – for contemporary debates take place in the shadow of Jasper's discussion.

"Primary" or true delusions are judged incomprehensible and meaningless, for Jaspers; they are the causal by-products of a dysfunctional brain. "Secondary" delusions, by contrast, possess meaningful content. This bifurcated analysis is situated within Jaspers's broader contrast between two kinds of explanation: that which follows the causal laws of the physical world, and *Verstehen*, the approach we employ to grasp the meanings linking psychological states and human action.

Added to these dualities is the complexity inherent in the

notions of meaningfulness and comprehensibility on which all discussions of these ideas must rest. These are each ambiguous and multi-stranded concepts. And they implicate incompatible philosophical accounts of meaning, that invite misunderstanding in the debate over whether observers – and their own subjects – can, or cannot, make sense of clinical delusions. Consider: the Norwegian word for "hedgehog" (*pinnsein*) may be incomprehensible to me because I do not know Norwegian, while comprehensible to anyone who does. So the intelligibility or comprehensibility of an utterance for the hearer is dependent on the knowledge possessed by that hearer. (That will be true for the speaker, as well, for I might voice "pinnsein" as a piece of nonsense.) From this, then, we would suppose that meaninglessness cannot be inferred in any straightforward way from incomprehensibility.

In addition, political realities affect who is found comprehensible (given "uptake," or accorded "semantic authority"), as philosophers of language have demonstrated.[1] It is the powerful who normally "determine what is said and sayable" (Frye 1983: 105), as it has been put. Since the profound powerlessness of those to whom clinical delusions are attributed can hardly be exaggerated, an extraordinarily delicate and generous approach seems to be called for here.[2]

This proposal involves not so much a definitive argument as a matter of assigning the burden of proof. In this respect, parallels can be seen with other controversies noted earlier. Some delusional content does seem to be meaningless, it will be argued here. Nonetheless, those denying meaningfulness to any or all delusions have the burden of persuading us of their case.

Philosophical theories of meaning seem to have bearing on the alleged meaninglessness of delusions. Donald Davidson and his followers hold that human minds are constituted to process thoughts in rational and coherent ways. So a principle of charity seems to encourage us to attribute meaningfulness to delusional ideas even when they elude comprehensibility. On philosophical accounts of meaning equating it with public use or intersubjective agreement such as Wittgenstein's, by contrast, meaningfulness can be nothing more than, and seems to reduce to, comprehensibility. Introducing the concept of solipsism and the category of a "private language" – this alternative viewpoint suggests what is at stake in Kant's notion of *sensus communis*, and the relation of meaning to use when use is understood as a necessarily collective activity.

These conceptual accounts of meaning each involve sweeping claims that seem to be too powerful for the multidimensional nature of clinical delusions, which apparently vary with respect to their meaningfulness and comprehensibility. Whether these theories can guide what we say about (some) delusions, or delusions instead stand as a refutation of such theories, is an issue addressed later in this chapter. For the present, and on the face of things, however, three positions are identifiable (they are dealt with in turn here): even when apparently comprehensible, true delusions are meaningless (Jaspers); whether or not there is apparent comprehensibility, meaningfulness can (and must) be attributed (Davidson's principle of charity); any meaningfulness that can be attributed to delusions depends on, and reduces to, comprehensibility (Wittgenstein).

Uses of language that are not standard and often not literal have long been linked to delusional thought. The role of metaphor in accounts of clinical delusions is a final issue affecting these questions about the meaningfulness and comprehensibility of delusions.

Jaspers's concept of *Verstehen*, the particular, distinctive method of understanding he thought appropriate in social sciences like psychiatry, is best seen in light of nineteenth-century German ideas about the social sciences, especially those of Wilhelm Dilthey (1833–1911) and Max Weber (1864–1920). Nature we explain, said Dilthey, but psychic life, we understand. The psychic life, and other phenomena related to the human sciences, must be accounted for "historically" or "genetically," restricting the historian to the perspective of his or her own time, and requiring a process of imaginative projection involving other people's mental states. The German "*Verstehen*" is literally "understanding." But for Dilthey and some who followed him, including Jaspers, it meant this special sense of understanding through a process of reliving, or empathic apprehension.

Both this specific notion of empathy and that of *Verstehen* appear to guide Jaspers in his analysis of the distinction between these two contrasting approaches. Due to such differences, the human being is not only a part of the material world where causal explanation applies, but something more elusive, involving meanings, and interpretation, Jaspers insists.

Of the process of empathy that yields the understanding called for in psychiatry, Jaspers describes "sinking ourselves into" the psychic situation in order to see "how one psychic event emerges from another" (Jaspers 1997: Vol. 1, 301). This account resembles what philosophers would later call adopting an intentional stance (Dennett) towards another person: inferring intention from speech and action, and predicting behavior from the attribution of mental states of belief and desire.

We need not accept that meaningful connections are non-causal to agree with much of what Jaspers says here.[3] He is surely right that human behavior may be approached in very different ways and differs, in that respect, from the phenomena encountered in the material world. Jaspers is also surely right that both forms of understanding are required in the study of human psychology and psychopathology. (And following in this tradition, some today adopt the hermeneutic approach to understanding delusions.[4])

"Primary" delusions are the exception to all this, for Jaspers. The empathic approach will be misplaced with them, for they possess no meaning. Much has been explained as meaningful which in fact was nothing of the kind, he says, sternly (Jaspers 1997: Vol. 1: 408). But primary experiences of delusions (or primary delusions) are in fact "quite alien modes of experience." They must be seen as ". . . largely incomprehensible, unreal and beyond our understanding" (Jaspers 1997: Vol.1, 98). This does not preclude treating the patient with empathy, but it emphasizes that no knowledge of the delusions will emerge from such an approach.

Jaspers's insistence that even seemingly comprehensible delusions may be meaningless is puzzling; some interpreters have supposed such remarks can only apply to delusions that are ostensibly incomprehensible, "bizarre," or "stark" (Ghaemi 2004, Klee 2004). "Someone has stolen my thoughts," "My wife has been replaced by an impostor," or "I am dead," may be meaningless as well as incomprehensible. Yet there are many more common delusions whose meaning seems entirely accessible: "Someone is following me," "Bugs are infesting my body," "I am immensely brilliant." Moreover, there seem to be intermediate cases, over which we want to acknowledge not so much incomprehensibility as ambiguity or perhaps indeterminacy over their meaning – we are uncertain whether we understand "I am God," "My soul is red," "I can read minds."[5]

Whatever its scope, Jaspers's attribution of incomprehensibility to a group of delusions has been influential, contributing, for instance, to the clinical practice of avoiding discussion of the content of delusions or hallucinations. And it has been supported not only by clinical observation (some delusions seem impossible to understand), but by argument. Jaspers denied meaningfulness to true delusions because he believed they were the causal by-products of a disordered brain, as well as on the basis of what he observed. (More recently, it has been argued that such delusions are meaningless because of their failure to cohere with either the rest of the patient's beliefs, or the meanings employed by those around him, as we'll see.)

Yet, the alleged meaninglessness of even bizarre and ostensibly unintelligible primary delusions has been called into question with cognitive approaches to treatment. The earlier practice of ignoring delusional content has increasingly been reversed, and interventions now include the identification and modification of the "faulty" basis of the patients' delusional beliefs through focus on the grounds for those beliefs, and the generation of alternative inferences from those grounds.[6]

Hallucinations, too, have been subject to recent re-evaluation along these lines.[7] What is hallucinated is not completely random, it has been pointed out; it is related in important ways to patients' personalities and to "the stresses that precipitate their psychoses" (Bentall 1990: 91).

There is certainly a way in which such thought content can be meaningfully connected with the patient's own, distinctive experience which is not entirely random. But non-randomness is not yet meaningfulness, and perceptual experiences are not quite like thoughts, beliefs and belief-like states that we *actively* entertain. (They are more like "unbidden" thoughts and ideas, of which we find ourselves passive recipients.) So although voices and other symptoms are depicted as "meaningful" and "significant" elements of experience and identity, we need to proceed cautiously here, and be guided by the words of patients themselves.

Looking back on an experience of psychosis, and explicitly rejecting a view like the Jasperian one, Colin Hambrook has written,

> I don't believe that the voices and hallucinations from which
> I've suffered in my life have merely been the result of a
> "biochemical imbalance," but have reflected a need from
> deep within myself to find myself.
>
> (Hambrook 1996: 148)

Hambrook's suffering possessed meaning or significance in serving as a spur to self-discovery and introspection, this implies.[8] Its importance to his life may have been profound. Yet here, meaningfulness appears to be used as it is when we say the clouds mean rain. Clouds are neither meaningful nor meaningless in any stronger semantic sense. They "mean" only as predictors of things to come.

By contrast, the narrator of the following example seems to use her words with full semantic meaning – but that meaning eludes us, her listeners and readers. Hospitalized for many years with psychosis, this woman spoke of (seemingly unlikely) changes in herself after a brain scan:

> Yes I have [changed]. My soul is red now. It used to be black.
> Everything is easier now. I can breathe. I can't explain it, but I

feel happy. I'm satisfied with myself . . . I'm burning with a
love for life. I accept life now.

(Torpor 2001: 198)

Much in this passage is entirely comprehensible. And the
part which isn't ("My soul is red now. It used to be black")
is perhaps a marginal case of a delusion. Yet it will serve
to illustrate that when she speaks of her soul – now red,
previously black – the "meaning" this woman finds in her
experience seems so lacking in shared connotations as to
be close to incomprehensible. The brain scan has been
imbued with strong, but idiosyncratically personal and private, significance. It is meaningful for her, while seemingly
impenetrable to us.

Those sentences comport with recognizable syntax, certainly, and so have superficial sense or coherence. Moreover,
contextual cues allow us to hazard the likely symbolic and
very positive connotations this woman attaches to the word
"red" (and negative ones to "black"). And these private
meanings are embedded among assertions that ring with
clarity and intelligibility ("I accept life now").

Are these assertions comprehensible? Partly, we want to
say; they comprise a mixture of more and less intelligible
elements. We all employ some "language" of private, idiosyncratic associations, whereby one idea has come to be
attached, for us, to another; moreover, encountering homo-
nyms, we all depend on context to ascertain meaning. Yet
when we use real, intersubjective language, these idio-
syncrasies are carefully (although effortlessly) excluded.
Perhaps, then, some clinical delusions differ not in reflecting
an idiosyncratic meaning-system, but in a failure to limit its
employment. A capability or set of capabilities involving

semantic agency, or what is sometimes called intentionality, seems to allow normal language users to recognize and "edit out" idiosyncratic meanings. If so, then a deficit in, or a disregard for, that capability occurs here: the patient cannot, or does not, mean in the normal way.

That delusions involve some such disturbance of the person's grasp of meanings, that is, their semantic agency or intentionality, has been proposed by several philosophers (Campbell 2001; Eilan 2001). One idea is that meaning what we say calls for coherence within a person's belief set. A related idea, introduced already, is that it involves adherence to meanings that are shared, and public. These interpretations, dealt with here in turn, connect with Davidsonian and Wittgensteinian presuppositions, respectively.

Meaninglessness as incoherence and the principle of charity

Naomi Eilan explores the meaninglessness of delusions in terms of a failure of fit between the person's belief, her other mental states, and her behavioral responses. Part of what is involved in meaning what we say requires this broader perspective (the very same broader perspective from which some theorists decide whether a person really believes what she says she believes). And incomprehensibility is sometimes attributed to a failure of coherence – when words are not matched by appropriate deeds, deeds by suitably linked intentions, beliefs and desires, and beliefs, thoughts, moods and attitudes by one another.

Incongruent words and deeds have frequently been associated with delusional thinking. Delusions are not action guiding, they are often "behaviorally inert," it has been pointed out; a kind of "double book-keeping" (Sass 1994) is engaged in. "Kings and Emperors, Popes and Redeemers engage . . . in quite banal work," reported Eugen Bleuler of his delusional inpatients in 1911, and,

> None of our generals has ever attempted to act in accordance with his imaginary rank and station.

(Bleuler 1950: 129)

A degree of behavioral inertia, and double bookkeeping beyond the ordinary apparently characterize some – not all – patients with delusions, it can be granted. And such incoherence will likely sometimes render their thought processes and actions opaque to the observer. What Eilan emphasizes is that such incoherence also suggests a failure of semantic agency or intentionality – the patient cannot mean the terms she uses in any normal way.

Qualification is called for here, for some behavioral inertia and double bookkeeping – or what are more commonly known as weakness of will, compartmentalization, self-deception, denial and the like – affect all of us. If this sort of incoherence characterizes delusions, delusional patients must exceed such normal incoherence to a marked degree. Some do, undoubtedly. Yet many patients maintain highly integrated cognitive systems; there is often coherence ("mood congruence") between delusional beliefs and other states, and patients with delusions act in many ways that are appropriate to the content of their delusions. At most, then, some delusions may be meaningless because they exhibit incoherence.

Philosophers writing about questions of belief and meaning often cite a "principle of charity," whereby meaningfulness is presumptively attributed to other people's assertions. When confronted with the seemingly incomprehensible "I keep two rhinoceroses in the refrigerator and squeeze one of them in the morning for breakfast," we have a restricted choice. We may either conclude that the speaker means "orange" when he says "rhinoceros," or that he has some very strange beliefs about the properties of rhinoceroses. That choice (over construing the relation among others' mental states) has been taken to indicate that there may not be any fact of the matter about what a person believes. There will always be alternative ways of balancing attributions of belief and meaning in our efforts to make sense of those around us.[9]

If such uncertainty stands in the way of determining the beliefs and meanings of other people, then it might be supposed we can never dismiss as meaningless the content of even the most obscure delusions. We're no worse off with regard to them, it might be said, than we are determining the meaningfulness of any assertions.

This is not a plausible position, however. Differences of opinion over the meaninglessness of delusions cannot be resolved by appeal to the principle of charity. First, those denying meaningful content to delusions might exempt them from that principle: if ordinary beliefs and meanings remain indeterminate in this way, delusional states, it can be insisted, are by contrast, determinately meaningless. Moreover, the principle of charity rests on a larger (and less charitable) presupposition – the idea that coherence and rational connections among one's beliefs are constitutive of having a mind, and being a thinker. The very reach of these ideas points to extreme implications and leaves us with constrained choices. If the beliefs of the person with delusions fail to form a coherent set, it seems we must choose between excluding him from personhood because he hasn't a mind at all, or finding fault with the Davidsonian principles.

Patients suffering from clinical delusions do have minds and are persons. If "proof" of this is necessary, it comes from pointing out, as others have, that these patients communicate intelligibly over many other matters unrelated to their delusions; that the relative rationality and coherence of even the patient with seemingly incomprehensible delusions more closely resemble the normal person's rationality and coherence than do, for example, those rendered unable to think or communicate through dementia, or patients with more severe forms of mental disorder (Broome 2004); and that the notions of having a mind and being a person admit of many different kinds and degrees (Klee 2004).

We may go further. Rather than resolving the question of their meaninglessness, the Davidsonian principles are arguably *defeated* by clinical delusions. Some delusions represent compelling counter-examples to these principles. Here are persons, with minds, palpably lacking the coherence and rational connections hitherto, mistakenly, judged essential to both. Even if this goes too far, and delusions are not convincing counter-examples, appeal to Davidsonian principles seems less than helpful in accounting for the phenomenon of delusional thought.

MEANINGLESSNESS AS SOLIPSISM

The key question about the deluded subject, John Campbell remarks, is ". . . whether the subject can be said to be holding on to the *ordinary meanings* of the terms used" (Campbell 2001: 95, emphasis added). Of bizarre primary delusions (such as the Capgras "My wife has been replaced by an impostor"), Campbell argues that part of the ordinary meanings of the terms used include our customary methods of verifying them. The usual grounds on which the thought

"My wife has been replaced by an impostor" would quickly be rejected as implausible have lost their force for the Capgras patient. The grounds on the basis of which a term is applied are part of what is involved in understanding and properly meaning it. With some bizarre and extreme delusions, the usual way of reasoning about ideas has been lost.

Whether "My soul is red now" demonstrates this degree of solipsistic meaninglessness, we saw, is not clear. But Campbell may be right that some delusions contain ideas not only incomprehensible to the hearer, but no longer meant by their subject due to a failure to recognize or be guided by the grounds for their use.

Everyday assumptions point to the psychotic's failure as a failure of commonality with the world of other perceivers and language users. So does the work of thinkers including Kant, as we saw earlier. To discern why the delusional status of some beliefs might lie with their not being (and perhaps not being able to be) shared, we need to further consider the idiosyncratic nature of some delusional thought.

In his later work Wittgenstein's previous criticisms of solipsism are provided with one particularly powerful supportive argument: he insists that an idiosyncratic "private language" could not be a proper language. Meaning and significance are tied to how words are used, and such use occurs within some linguistic community. Only a mistaken conception of meaning could permit us to envision the possibility of a "language" for one person only – that is, a pseudo language such as is presupposed by the doctrine of solipsism. There, meaning and reference would involve something grander, and something more interior to the subject, than what groups of people do.

But Wittgenstein offers a different picture of communication. The rules for correctly employing and comprehending meaning are community practices (what groups of people do), relying finally on the brute and inexplicable fact that our judgements concur or "agree" – not because we have agreed, but because they just do. The social and intersubjective nature of language use, thought and judgement, according to this understanding, depicts thinkers grasping the rules governing the use of a concept in its applications and its role in thought sequences through a combination of mimicry and responding to correction by others ("That's not red, that's purple").[10] If language use and semantic agency depend on intersubjective agreement this way, then – presupposing as it must a "language" for one, and meanings that are unshared – solipsism is impossible. And if delusions involve meanings that are also solipsistically idiosyncratic, they will also be on that account meaningless.

What must be kept in mind as we evaluate the Wittgensteinian doctrine in relation to delusions, is that meaningfulness and intelligibility are each matters of degree. "My soul is red" can be seen as an intermediate case, for example; it is partially comprehensible. The position that delusions involve unshared meanings is compatible with the observation that particular delusions vary in the degree to which they are meaningless and incomprehensible.

Emphasizing the kind of meanings that are lost by the delusional patient, Campbell and Eilan invoke another Wittgensteinian notion. "Framework principles" are shared, but also implicit and ungrounded assumptions and expectations about the world (that I have two hands is an example). Part of the ordinary meanings of words, it is these that the delusional patient is said to have lost. Others have also proposed that the shared meanings eluding the person with delusions are the ones that are vital to our pre-reflexive grasp of the world. They have been described as "axioms of everyday life" (Stenghellini) that include non-propositional knowledge, and "bedrock certainties" (Rhodes and Gipps) that are not held for reasons, and require no justification.

If loss of pre-reflexive certainties that are not grounded in reasons is implicated in the apparent meaninglessness of some delusions, then Jaspers may have been right in pointing to true delusions as fundamentally meaningless. But this set of ideas also seems too sweeping for the range and variety of delusional states. Even the simple, bizarre delusions Campbell uses as examples may not involve loss of pre-reflexive assumptions; such explanations of seemingly incomprehensible delusions ("My husband has been replaced by an impostor") are apparently belied by the way patients with these delusions still proceed unexceptionally in many ways that presuppose adherence to shared assumptions or framework principles. A grasp of the world is retained in any number of practical situations, allowing patients to keep, as Sass observed, a quite accurate sense of their actual circumstances. If such profound and global deficits were involved, it is difficult to explain how this could be done. Rather than applying to even bizarre and apparently incomprehensible delusions, this description of a loss of pre-reflexive assumptions better fits more severely disordered minds: those with the cognitive disarray of advanced dementia, for example.[11]

For ordinary and comprehensible delusions, moreover, such accounts seem unnecessary. Explanation of common or garden-variety delusions ("Someone is following me," "Bugs are infesting my body," "I am immensely brilliant") often seem to rest on little beyond the assumptions that would likely be shared by others. The particular, unshared bases for these assertions look to be distorted interpretations of ambiguous cues: from "she is looking at me," to "someone is following me"; from "there are spots on my skin," to "bugs are infesting me"; and from "they have failed to recognize my superior qualities," to "I am immensely brilliant." The problem with each of the above delusional beliefs ("someone is following me" etc.) lies not with a failure to adhere to pre-reflexive assumptions, or even to widely agreed rules of evidence or grounding. Instead, it seems to lie with the application of those rules to particular, often ambiguous, observations and experiences.

Appeals to a loss of implicit (pre-reflexive or groundwork) beliefs seem to be unpersuasive then, whether as explanations of (all) bizarre delusions, or of more everyday ones.

Meaning and metaphor

John Perceval's famous *Narrative on the Treatment Experienced by a Gentleman during a State of Mental Derangement* (1840) reminds us of the long-observed clinical association between delusional thought and non-literal meaning. After describing some of the delusions which he had experienced when ill, Perceval remarks:

> I suspect that many of the delusions which I labored under, and which other insane persons labour under, consist in their mistaking a figurative or poetic form of speech for a literal one. . . .

Observing the other inmates of the asylum, he goes on:

> . . . you will hear one lunatic declare that he is made of iron, and that nothing can break him; another that he is a china vessel, and that he runs in danger of being destroyed every minute. The meaning of the spirit is, that this man is strong as

iron, the other frail as an earthen vessel; but the lunatic takes
the literal sense, and his imagination not being under his own
control, he in a manner feels it.

(These passages are quoted in Kaplan 1964: 243)

Perceval's notion that the patient is unable to employ the
distinction between literal and non-literal language, and that
delusions become comprehensible when we acknowledge
their non-literal meaning, has echoes in some recent research.
Patients with schizophrenia perform less well at discerning
metaphorical from literal meaning, for example.[12, 13] And the
apparent frequency of metaphor in delusional thinking has
prompted several hypotheses. Alarming anomalous experience may have disabled capabilities involving metaphor and
lead to a process of "slipping from metaphor to literal belief"
(Rhodes and Jakes 2004: 10). Symbolic meanings may have
come to appear "self-subsistent" – leading psychotics to
conclude "the meaning was inherent in the object, or . . .
indicated or revealed to them by some cosmic order or other
agent" (Brett 2002: 328–9).

Perceval's examples involve the most elementary confu-
sions between seemingly false empirical claims ("I am made
of iron") and their metaphorical or figurative interpretation
(this man is strong as iron). Shared rules govern the literal use
of empirical concepts like "iron," and even the metaphors
associated with them.[14] In cases such as those Perceval
gives, he may be right. But even simple observational terms
such as "red," as we saw earlier, may be imbued with impenetrable idiosyncratic connotations that make any "translation"
between figurative and literal impossible for observers.

In addition, the non-empirical content that is so often
the stuff of delusions cannot readily be judged this way.

Delusional ideas with metaphysical, religious, ideological or spiritual content are at once more abstract and – if they have literal uses at all – less strictly guided by rules to separate literal from other uses. Schreber insists that the stuff of his delusions which "exceed human understanding" can be expressed only in images and similes, as we saw, and it is a view shared by some analyses of all religious language.[15] In his ebullient and compelling diaries (1995), Nijinsky repeatedly remarks that he is God. "I am God" may be intended as mere metaphor (representing omniscience, perhaps, or some other perfection). But to know how the assertion would be employed more literally, we would need to know about the conception of God adhered to in his sub-community. And if he is employing an entirely idiosyncratic association, of course, even this will not help us understand.

Further challenging Perceval's hypothesis are the "subjunctifiers" used to qualify reports of inner states, noted earlier, which often alert us to non-literal usage. But if those who describe their delusions with care employ qualifications this way, then rather than incapable of separating more and less figurative usage, they seem almost preternaturally alert to that distinction.

At most, then, some delusions might reflect confusion between literal and non-literal meanings as Perceval believed. Others will be incomprehensible due to the idiosyncratic connotations involved – whether literal or metaphorical. For metaphors can be as shared and public as literal meanings.[16] (They are the very stuff of everyday communication, indeed; we seem to need, and live by, shared metaphors.[17]) Seemingly incomprehensible delusions may reflect non-literal language that is idiosyncratic and unshared.

The relation between delusions and non-literal meaning is explored in R. D. Laing's *Divided Self* (1959). Laing shared with Jung the conviction that the schizophrenic's utterances contain meaning, quoting with approval Jung's statement that "the schizophrenic ceases to be schizophrenic when he meets someone by whom he feels understood" (Laing 1959: 165).[18]

Instead of depicting the expression of any universal, symbolic language, however, as Jung had done, Laing portrays a communicator often intent on sowing confusion. At the heart of our difficulty making sense of some delusional and psychotic responses lies language that is not only elliptical and figurative, but also purposefully unintelligible.[19]

It may be hard to defend, but this provocative description at least reminds us of the many things we can, and do, do with words. Yet to his depiction of the schizophrenic as a wily manipulator, Laing adds a picture of some psychotic patients that is closer to Jaspers's, and a notion of the hermeneutic task that is nearer Freud's. Trapped within the symbolic, and private, "language" of their obscure thoughts and speech, some patients need the help of an interpreter. The meaning of those thoughts and speech cannot be deciphered without the background information patients provide, yet patients cannot extricate their meaning alone. Audaciously, Laing explains to us what his patient Julie could mean by her seemingly incomprehensible, delusional assertions. Some statements, as he puts it, ". . . are often quite impossible to fathom without the patient decoding them for us" (Laing 1959: 192).

This decoding is not an outcome of the patients' own semantic agency in any ordinary way, however. The person playing at being mad to avoid being held responsible for his words exhibits such ordinary agency. In contrast, Laing's patient Julie, whose garbled ideas and speech he has to interpret using the shreds and patches of information he can ascertain about her life and experience, exhibits speech more fundamentally meaningless. While they are the product of her situation, Julie's claims are meaningless to the patient herself. They are not indicative of semantic agency, however comprehensible they can be made to be by her interpreter.

The paranoid's delusional misapprehension that he is being followed may be ungrounded, but it is comprehensible. And many such delusions are apparently meaningful, as well. Yet other delusions may not be, and Kant's *sensus communis* seems to apply here. In some instances, delusions rest on terms that are unshared, the product of "private languages" sufficiently idiosyncratic that they are not real languages. They can be subject to hermeneutic interpretation of the sort provided by Laing, granting them some limited, and different, kind of sense. But we understand why Jaspers denied that status to many such ideas when they are so obscure, because the usual relation is absent here by which, whether literally or figuratively, we mean our ideas.

Clinical delusions sometimes exhibit incomprehensibility and even meaninglessness, then. But they do so in a range of ways and to different degrees. And the blanket application of theories of meaning fails to capture the variety and nuanced differences to be found in clinical phenomena. Moreover no delusions, however incomprehensible, approach the meaninglessness wrought by more severe conditions, the cognitive disintegration of dementia or the thought disorder, and mute inaccessibility of some extreme instances of psychosis.

Delusions as Shared: *folies à deux* and the
Madness of Crowds

Five

When emphasis is placed on intersubjective agreement in identifying the way clinical delusions contravene our epistemic values, as it was in the previous chapter, something of a puzzle begins to emerge. On the one hand, it is precisely the solipsistic, and idiosyncratically "private" nature of some states that makes us think of them as delusional. Yet in *folie à deux*, one person is described as inducing or effecting delusional states in another. And, acknowledging the so-called "madness of crowds," the effects of social contagion on belief states, affect and behavior have long been observed. Some unshared beliefs seem to be delusional because they are solipsistic then, but so also are shared beliefs when they result from social contagion.

Unshared ideas need not be delusional, of course – as the hypotheses of the lonely visionary thinker illustrate. But when ideas arise from idiosyncratic, unshared meanings, we saw, they fail to conform with our notions of proper semantic agency. So while something seems right about Kant's assertion that it is the possession of *sensus communis* that separates normal from delusional thought, some shared ideas prompted by those around us have been judged the essence of mindless delusional irrationality.

The ideas spread by way of such contagions are often judged dangerous. They are also wanting in other respects, however: they are ill-grounded and often implausible notions, and their means of transmission, particularly, seems contrary to our norms of rationality.

FOLIES À DEUX

The patient in the clinic is an individual: that is presupposed, in the prevailing model of psychiatry within which our term "clinical delusion" is understood. And many delusions arise from the patient's distinctive personal and natural history and particular vulnerabilities (they may be said to be "idiopathic" or "endogenous" in this respect). Yet, delusions also result solely, or at least primarily, from the effect of groups of people. Before turning to the delusions brought about this way, we must look at the intermediate cases – those resulting from intimate or close contact with others.

Folies à deux involve the transfer of psychotic symptoms, primarily delusions, from one individual to another. (It has been proposed that the term "delusion" is inapplicable for the ideas of the second individual.[1] But neither phenomenological nor clinical descriptions recognize this convention.) Their most obvious feature is the shared, indeed identical, delusional content. Persecutory and grandiose themes have been found to predominate, but many others occur as well, including the delusional parasitosis described earlier (see p. 33), when first mother and then grown son believed themselves invaded by microscopic insects.

Several additional features have since the nineteenth century been used to distinguish this condition. The frequently observed social isolation of the pair or social group is one of these. Others are its recurrence in intimate relationships, such as those between husband and wife, or mother and daughter; the process by which one partner seems to "infect" the other, and the entrenched quality of the belief system that makes it hard to treat even when pairs are separated.

Its commonness among family members, and the evidence of other psychopathology in the secondary partner that may indicate a susceptibility factor, have given rise to much speculation over the origin of folie à deux. Rather than the outcome of social interaction with an intimate made more potent by social isolation, for example, some analyses have proposed that partners share the same genetically driven psychiatric illness or tendency.[2] Debates over the respective contributions of genetic and social ingredients of this condition need not concern us, however. It is not, nor could it plausibly be, proposed that these delusional ideas have arisen coincidentally. The social aspect is, as seems apparent, a necessary condition, if not a sufficient one, for the presence of delusions with particular, identical, content. The sometimes bizarre, often implausible ideas that are found in these cases make them otherwise indistinguishable from many other delusions. So strong is their shared belief about infestation, for example, that patients with delusional parasitosis as folies à deux are described as insistently denying any psychiatric explanation of their complaints and seeking dermatological help instead.[3]

These shared convictions are thus maintained the way many other delusions are, and are indistinguishable from them in their thematic content. The next question is whether they are acquired any differently from usual. Efforts have been made to sort the way these ideas become part of the second patient's belief system. Folie imposée suggests a passive recipient in the secondary patient and it has been distinguished from folie communiquée, when the recipient actively engages with the ideas, only accepting them after initial resistance. In addition, are cases of more mutual influence, *induction reciproque*, or *division du travail*.[4] But to situate the question of how such delusional ideas are acquired, we need to keep in mind how ideas are transferred in normal and everyday instances.

Other people produce changes in our ideas, beliefs and attitudes, and engender convictions in us. This, in all its multitude of forms, is what is known as normal social learning. And allowing other people to influence us, through demonstration, example, rational persuasion, emotional appeal, and so on, is central to our human way of life and to our norms of rationality. (It is, in varying degrees, normative as well as statistically normal.) Moreover, this will often be especially true if those others are intimates. Trust exceeding that extended to strangers is generally extended to intimates. We know better the reliability of intimates as sources, and so quite reasonably, we generally trust them more – except when, knowing them to be unreliable, we (judiciously) trust them less. In addition, intimates usually communicate directly with us – to demonstrate, confirm, remind, affirm, reveal, support and persuade.

In light of the ways of normal (and normative) social learning, particularly evident among intimates, the inducing of an idea in one person by another in *folie à deux* seems likely to conform to epistemic norms governing the acquisition of those states: their mode of transfer will be unexceptional. Corresponding to the subcategories identified above, we recognize learning through being informed (*folie imposée*), being persuaded in the face of resistance (*folie communiquée*), and working more mutually towards a conclusion (*induction reciproque* or *division du travail*). If the beliefs of *folies à deux* involve irrational or delusional states, their irrationality will likely lie not in the way they have been acquired but in their content and grounding, and in the manner in which they are maintained.

Both *folies à deux* and the group delusions to which we'll next turn involve the influence of other people. In this respect they contrast sharply with many other clinical delusions. In contrast also to *folies à deux*, however, group delusions strictly so called are sometimes distinguished by their means of transmission, apparently infecting people through a process analogous to the transmission of contagious bodily diseases and infections. Here, then, although they are little understood, are a different kind of delusion altogether.

GROUP DELUSIONS AND THE MADNESS OF CROWDS

Recognition that groups and crowds engender ideas in these strange ways has a long history, although not one widely remembered today.[5] Mobs, crowds, groups – others, more generally – affect individual belief states. And the relation of these effects to clinical delusional states and other forms of irrationality was a subject of considerable interest during earlier times.[6]

To understand how these effects of groups on individuals were construed, and why "delusion" was the word chosen, we need a little history of ideas from between the first third of the nineteenth century and the end of the first quarter of the twentieth – between Scottish faculty psychologist Dugald Stewart writing in 1827, and Freud's *Group Psychology and the Analysis of the Ego* (1922), let us say. Stewart observes that the contagious nature of convulsions, of hysteric disorders, of panics, and of "all the different kinds of enthusiasm," are commonly referred by medical writers to the principle of Imitation. But, among these various phenomena, he goes on:

> ... there are some which depend also on a combination
> of very powerful causes of another description; – on the
> influence, for example, of Imagination, and of those passions
> which are apt to be kindled wherever men are assembled in
> a crowd: ... As bodily affections seem to be, in certain cases,
> contagious, where they are altogether unaccompanied by
> any mental passion or emotion, so, on the other hand, the
> passions and emotions felt, or supposed to be felt by one
> individual, have a tendency to spread among his companions,
> even without the intervention of any external expression
> manifested in the appearance ... When ... the feelings of
> a crowd are in unison ... the effect is likely to be incalculably
> great; the mind at once acting on the body, and the body
> re-acting on the mind, while the influence of each is
> manifested by the inexplicable contagion of sympathetic
> imitation.
>
> (Quoted in Hunter and Macalpine 1982: 642)

Stewart's "inexplicable contagion of sympathetic imitation" is what became known as the madness of crowds, and each element – its inexplicability, its rapid spread, and its link to some capacity of sympathetic imitation – remains essential to later accounts of the delusions that resulted. Writing soon after Stewart, the German medical historian J. F. C. Hecker drew very similar conclusions, speaking of the hypnotic effects of imitation, compassion and sympathy, which he calls a "common bond of union among human beings." To the instinct of imitation, he remarks, is united "a loss of all power over the will" (Hecker 1846: 139).[7] Contagions bypass any way we might normally acquire beliefs.

Mackay's work, quoted earlier, was little more than a compendium of curious cases, hinting at these mysterious processes. It was the French thinkers, who at the end of the nineteenth century refined the notion of the group mind and its hypnotic effects on group psychology. With their ideas of suggestion and contagion, Tarde and LeBon provided the foundations for Freud's famous analysis. Freud quotes with approval LeBon's assertion that "[w]hoever be the individuals that compose it, however like or unlike be their mode of life, their occupations, their character, or their intelligence, the fact that they have been transformed into a group puts them in possession of a sort of collective mind which makes them feel, think, and act in a manner quite different from that in which each individual of them would . . . were he in a state of isolation"(Freud 1959/1922: 5). The features of groups that allow what is heterogeneous to be submerged in what is homogenous, as Freud paraphrases LeBon, include a disinhibition, a contagious communication between group members, and heightened suggestibility in each group member.

To these ideas about "contagious communication" as the basis of group delusions, Freud added his own mix. Suggestibility produces the contagion that is engendered by group membership and leads groups to disinhibited actions displaying "primitive" unconscious processes (Freud 1959/1922: 7). Here, Freud emphasizes the irrational nature of these beliefs because they come from the unconscious, characterized by the illogic of infantile, "primary process" thinking.

Also helpful is the work of Emile Durkheim, writing twenty years earlier than Freud. (Le Suicide was first published in 1897.) With a profound interest in imitative behavior, Durkheim was at the same time cautious over his contemporaries' reliance on the mysterious notion of the hypnotic effects of group minds on individual behavior. He provides a useful guide to the spread of interpersonal "infection" in the particular case of historical instances of apparently contagious suicides. Much of Durkheim's data is anecdotal at best. But, he has offered what remains one of the clearest and most precise discussions of imitative "mass" behavior, distinguishing between actions resulting from rational processes and those from the contagious effects of mimetic or imitative tendencies. Not all group-engendered behavior need involve the particular irrational elements identified as social contagion, Durkheim recognized. And this recognition allows him to craft an analytic definition of contagiously wrought action, not since bested: "the immediate antecedent of an act is the representation of a like act, previously performed by someone else; with *no explicit or implicit mental operation* which bears upon the intrinsic nature of the act reproduced intervening between representation and execution" (Durkheim 1951: 129n, emphasis added).

By pointing to the absence of explicit or implicit mental operations here, Durkheim intends the absence of operations *within conscious awareness*, of course. He was not precluding the machinations of non-conscious ("sub-personal," "non-doxastic") systems and, indeed, seems to anticipate the "modern cognitive unconscious" (Frankish) comprising belief states that are inaccessible to conscious awareness, effort or critical evaluation.

More recent theorizing, including Freud's, has sketched the added ingredients of group-engendered contagion by acknowledging suggestibility to be an individual trait or liability. In the case of a suggestion, Freud had earlier observed, "an idea is aroused in another's brain which is not examined in regard to its origin but is accepted just as though it had arisen spontaneously in that brain" (Freud 1959/1922: 20). Suggestibility refers to an individual tendency to bypass the process of critical evaluation of a new idea's origin before accepting it. Durkheim emphasizes behavior, and the absence of reflection intervening between observing and imitating an action. Freud's notion is broader, focused on the tendency to adopt uncritically not only impulses to act, but other cognitive states. Yet both accounts stress the non-rational way belief states (and hence the actions to which they give rise) are acquired. Whether or not irrationality attaches to the content of these belief states, or the way they are maintained, their acquisition transgresses the epistemic norms governing social learning. (Although it is not our immediate concern here, brainwashing, of course, seems to do the same.[8])

Humans are creatures of imitation and mimicry. We tend to adopt the behavior of others, as well as absorbing their ideas and feelings, and these effects regularly occur outside of conscious awareness. (Recent findings about the function of the so-called mirror neurons have confirmed the extent and importance of this claim.[9]) The mimetic sub-capabilities making possible both imitation and suggestibility would seem to be the same or similar ones. The tendency to readily and unwittingly accept, adopt or internalize stimuli, such as ideas, affects and behavioral responses, from outside the self is a working definition that encompasses both capabilities. (This definition is sufficiently broad to accommodate the several sub-traits making up suggestibility, and the considerable variation between individuals in their possession of these traits, both revealed through experimental studies.[10])

Social, communicative and probably evolutionary advantages attach to possession of these mimetic tendencies – even though such ready absorption will be undesirably uncritical. The range of beliefs and responses deriving from forms of social contagion seems likely vast, even illimitable. Describing all the false, foolish and unreasonable beliefs and ideas alleged to be "delusional" that occur outside the clinic, including many with an ideological cast, would require not one volume but many, as Mackay rightly recognized, and they are well beyond the scope of the present discussion. But our interest in social contagion is narrower. It concerns the hypothesis that some clinical delusions are the result – if not solely, then at least significantly – of social contagion. Many other delusions may owe more to these mysterious forms of transmission than has hitherto been recognized, even within the clinic. Here, however, the case is made for just one kind, the delusional conviction of those suffering eating disorders that their body is too fat, or otherwise unacceptable.

EATING DISORDERS AND THE CULT OF THINNESS

The status of the mistaken and dangerous conviction that one is undesirably fat as delusional, rather than delusion-like or an overvalued idea, is contested.[11] So is the relation of these to other disorders.[12] But such a conviction nonetheless seems to be an almost invariable cognitive accompaniment of eating disorder as it occurs in Western cultures, whatever further symptoms that disorder exhibits, so we can fairly safely presume that some at least of these convictions fit the loose category of delusion employed here.

Not all these mistaken beliefs about one's size will fall into the class of ideas resulting from social contagion.[13] Many, presumably, will have been acquired by way of more normal social learning. Works such as Sharlene Nagy Hesse-Biber's *The Cult of Thinness* (2007) provide first-hand accounts of eating disorder implicating all the usual ways ideas are transmitted from one person to another – persuasion, discussion, conscious imitation, and so on. The processes leading to what may have become delusional convictions are unsurprising, even rational, in these descriptions: a mother's persuasion and bullying, a desire to emulate an admired (slender) acquaintance, a way to realize greater control of one's life, or to appeal to men. But we can hardly expect those affected by such social contagion to be aware of being so affected; first-person accounts will of course fail to acknowledge that influence.

Hesse-Biber's emphasis on the societal obsession with thinness that engenders eating disorders in young women hints at the more subliminal elements contributing to the "epidemic" she describes. The sources of this cult of thinness are all around us, and sometimes subtly influential: American women are exhorted to strive for a physical idea; where, as she says, "Fat represents moral failure, the inability to delay gratification, poor impulse control, greed, and self-indulgence"; the slim figure has come to represent health; and market interests exploit women's insecurities about their looks.[14] In addition to the influence of institutions that reward conformity to such values, these considerations lead Hesse-Biber to describe as a "cult" the behavior of young women today, many of whom will succumb to eating disorders.[15] Cults, she says, involve ritualistic performance (here, anorexia, bulimia and compulsive exercise) and obsession with a goal or ideal (thinness). The use of the term "cult" is suggestive, for it reminds us that cults are groups, whose members influence one another. Anorexia and bulimia are predominantly women's disorders, and Hesse-Biber remarks that being female is the primary criterion for membership in the "cult of thinness." This is also illuminating, because the influence of several aspects of our culture such as the Internet do not require face-to-face contact or interpersonal exchange.

Social epidemics harken back to the original infectious-disease connotations of "epidemic," that implicate less conscious, and more obscure, forms of contagion whereby pathologies are unwittingly "caught" by those affected. That said, the effect of other people will be unlikely a sufficient condition for the spread of the disorder, even while it is necessary. (This, we saw, was so with *folies à deux*, as well.) Even when they are attributed to the influence of groups, self-destructive behavioral pathologies such as eating disorders are widely understood to occur only in vulnerable individuals with particular predisposing susceptibility or risk factors.[16]

In many instances, the epidemic spread of self-destructive disorders may be explained solely in terms of normal social learning. However, the elusive, sub-personal nature of the transfer of ideas in which we are interested must by its nature elude assessments as to its prevalence. As soon as such influence was noticed, it would be indistinguishable from more normal learning. At best, perhaps, to illustrate these effects, we will discover correlations linking exposure to subtle sources of cultural influence, on the one hand, and consequent changes in ideas about body image, on the other.

One such account, reported by a sociologist studying women through "pro anorexia" websites, describes the way exposure to such influences led to unexpected and unwelcome changes in her own awareness and attitudes. Employing "virtual ethnographic" methods, this researcher's goal was to engage in "covert participant observation, to understand the online subculture of pro-ana sites and (anorexic) individual's online profiles" (Gailey 2009: 96). This included recording her responses to what she viewed while collecting information from blogs, posts, bulletins, discussion forums, comments, and profiles, and of these responses she writes:

. . . After spending several months exploring pages and reading blogs, I . . . had to limit how much time I spent viewing and reading their blogs, comments, and posts because *I too* found myself becoming increasingly fixated on my own eating and exercising habits . . . staring at images of emaciated models for several hours a night and reading about how awful it is to be fat does influence one who already has disordered eating tendencies. Therefore I . . . decided that in order to overcome the negative reactions I experienced with my own eating I had to limit the amount of time I spent reading and collecting information each week.

(Gailey 2009: 97, emphasis added)

The author admits to a predisposing factor: only by restricting her exposure to these materials was she able to avoid letting her tendencies towards eating disorder reach clinical proportions. This passage lays bare the socially contagious aspects of eating disorders very clearly, nonetheless. Exposure to those ideas and images, in combination with innate mimetic tendencies, altered her attitudes towards her own body in ways that bypassed the degree of awareness and control we associate with normal learning and reasonable ways to acquire beliefs.

MIMETIC TENDENCIES AND THE "SPACE OF REASONS"

Our extensive, unlearned human imitative capabilities have been seen to indicate that imitation is "default social behavior" and the "social glue" underlying all human inter-subjectivity (Dijksterhuis 2005: 208). A similar point applies to suggestibility: without it, such intersubjectivity, and much cooperative effort, seem likely to be diminished or defective.[17] Assertions about widespread, mimetic responses transmitted outside the normal communicative modalities have prompted recent discussions, however, that diminish or reduce the person-centered focus of any and all human action and decision. For example, it is common to speak of "memes" finding hosts rather than people acting intentionally, and to dismiss all talk of rational action as loose and misleading folk psychology.

This reductionistic way of looking at things is belied by the fact that even cases of mimicry will sometimes, and to greater or lesser degrees, depend on separate self-conscious and intentional efforts, and even, sometimes, efforts at imitation. Acting from some particular, idiosyncratic reason, as well as acting in order to imitate, are both quite different from the unwitting adoption of the same course of action.[18] We do, and should, distinguish these very different communicative modes.

That mimicry and imitation themselves come in each form is the first point to be acknowledged. Not only are there brief behavioral responses (such as yawning, and laughing) that can occur either spontaneously by contagion or imitation, or as the result of intentional and self-conscious action (whether its goal is imitation or not). In addition, most complex behavior will likely involve a combination of unbidden and intentional responses. Trends in fashion are an often-cited manifestation of socially contagious ideas and inclinations. We may even include the Werther-inspired yellow pants, blue jackets and open-necked shirts said to have became the fashion in Germany in the 1770s following the publication of Goethe's *Sorrows of Young Werther*. To be drawn to Werther-inspired clothes from observing them on others may have been the result of mindless social contagion; to purchase and wear those outfits, not. And it would seem that much apparently imitative behavior will call for such combinations of mindful and mindless activity.

More importantly, even when the conscious, intentional states required for the usual effect of one person on another are bypassed due to social contagion, this does not indicate that our more customary forms of rational persuasion and social learning are wrongly understood. Nor does it imply that we cannot – or should not – preserve the normative distinction between transmission through forms of social learning accessible to conscious monitoring (learning which we can intend, decide, resolve and choose to resist, for example) and behavior that is "caught" like an infectious disease. Imitation and suggestibility may play a larger part in the way people affect others than has hitherto been realized. Arguably, these traits must be very common – if only as a precondition for the "agreements in judgement" (Wittgenstein 1969) that make possible the trademark intersubjectivity that is our human way of life. But acknowledgement that imitation and suggestibility may be essential preconditions of human social behavior leaves untouched normative assessments of apparently delusional ideas brought about through social contagion or imitation. And these same arguments are as applicable to the contagious transfer of ideas and attitudes as they are to impulses to behave. The acquisition of cognitive content from other people through normal social learning that allows us to critically evaluate and on that basis decide to accept or reject those ideas, remains a mode of exchange better fitted to our epistemic values and ideals.

Some group-engendered states are appropriately included in an inventory of delusions because, resulting from social contagion, they transgress our epistemic norms. (When they involve self-destructive impulses and behavior they also contrave mental health norms in other ways.) The eating disorders that were the focus of this discussion represent a particularly vivid example because cultural values around thinness are so pervasive. But similar claims can be made for other forms of self-destructive disorder treated in the clinic, including suicidality. (Moreover, the social contagion analysis proposed here likely extends to the pervasive ideologies that seem to foster and nourish many paranoid delusions.)

Perhaps few ideas acquired through social contagion are delusional, and few self-destructive ideas are acquired through the kind of social contagion described – the facts here, as we saw, must of necessity be elusive. But the convictions of the anorexic who, subliminally influenced by pervasive cultural stereotypes, starves herself because she believes she is abhorrently fat, can very plausibly be understood this way.[19]

Spiritual Delusions – Religious,
Metaphysical, Ideological

Six

Religious and more broadly non-natural or "metaphysical"
themes are some of the commonest in a variety of delusions.[1]
(For brevity, we can from henceforth call these "spiritual"
ideas.) And they present a distinctive set of epistemic challenges because of their subject matter. Recent research, none
entirely successful, has sought to show how such delusions
differ from normal religious belief (closely parallel efforts also
attempt to distinguish religious and spiritual experience more
generally understood from psychotic experience). The ways
spiritual delusions are acquired have received little attention.
Yet several of these – in particular, both delusions resulting from the intuitive apprehension of meaning, described
as delusional perception (Chapter 2), and those acquired
through social contagion – fail to comport with epistemic
norms. Although many spiritual delusions are characterized
by the first of these aberrant means of acquisition, and others
perhaps ought to be characterized by the second, this hardly
serves, it is concluded here, to distinguish even these from
many more ordinary religious convictions.

RELIGIOUS AND METAPHYSICAL
DELUSIONS – SUBJECT MATTER

The peculiar nature of spiritual delusions is easily exposed by a standard (and influential) definition of delusion.

> A false personal belief based on incorrect inference about external reality and firmly sustained in spite of what almost everyone else believes and in spite of what constitutes incontrovertible and obvious proof or evidence to the contrary. The belief is not one ordinarily accepted by other members of the person's culture or subculture (i.e. [e.g.], it is not an article of religious faith). When a false belief involves an extreme value judgment, it is regarded as a delusion only when the judgment is so extreme as to defy credibility.[2]

Several difficulties beset definitions such as this that stress the falsity of the beliefs involved in delusion. Some delusions even about factual matters ("external reality") are or may be true. And many delusions seem not to be about factual matters at all, including those with religious, spiritual, ideological or metaphysical content.

Delusions are often palpably false, by any measure. Clamembault's syndrome, where the patient suffers the delusion that a total stranger is in love with her, cannot be true – nor can those incomprehensibly self-contradictory delusional thoughts such as the Cotard idea that "I am dead." Yet some states, while considered delusional, nonetheless concern something that is true. (The patient's conviction of her husband's infidelity may be delusional not because it is not in some cases accurate, as Jaspers has pointed out, but because it is improperly grounded.) However, the second problem is our subject here. The content of many delusions involves spiritual matters – more like Nijinsky's "I am God" than like

"A stranger is in love with me" or "I am dead." From the ubiquity of spiritual themes in clinical delusions, and of ideological and other value judgements that similarly evade ordinary verification, we might be inclined to conclude that relatively few delusions possess truth value, and this represents a major limitation in definitions such as the one just quoted.

Definitions of that kind actually exclude two common kinds of delusional content. Spiritual assertions often purport to represent the outside – although non-material – world. But there are also many clinical delusions about inner experience, such as "I feel that it is not me who is thinking," or "My thoughts are not thought by me."[3] These delusions are as immune from evaluation as to truth or falsity, although differently, as those of the person who says "I am God."

For Manfred Spitzer, delusion reflects a failure to separate the appropriate "incorrigibility" that marks everyone's assertions about their ordinary inner states (such as "I feel sad" or "have a headache"), from the corrigibility that accompanies speech about things and events in the public world, where other people can correct or confirm what we say. Deluded people attach incorrigibility to their beliefs about external reality (Spitzer 1990). This is not to deny all sense to assertions about internal reality. "I feel that it is not me who is thinking," may have some kind of meaning for the speaker. But such assertions have a different epistemological status that prevents us from calling them delusions, Spitzer insists. They are distinguished from delusions proper as "disturbances of the I" or "disturbances of experience" (German *Ichstörungen*) which do not admit of intersubjective confirmation and disconfirmation.

This uncompromising notion of incorrigibility returns us to the depiction of the mind as an inner theater whose events are described in first-person report, rejected by Wittgenstein. And whether we need to redraw the boundaries so that delusions proper only involve ideas about publicly verifiable "external reality" may depend on how convinced we are by the alternative, Wittgensteinian model of language as essentially public and shared.

The present chapter, however, concerns ideas about a reality that is external rather than internal. These ideas seem to reflect the obverse of the epistemic problems introduced by delusional content about inner states. Rather than too internal, religious, metaphysical and spiritual ideas – inasmuch as they are construed as about a transcendent or supernatural reality – are almost too external. Their verification, even when these rest on shared, public and cooperative efforts, may be supposed to exceed our limited human capabilities. How could we mere mortals know whether or not Nijinsky was God, for example?

While some spiritual delusions are clearly intended more literally, many apparently make claim to symbolic or figurative meaning. If we accept that beliefs about supernatural matters can be neither true nor false, we must still consider their force and applicability as metaphorical language. Recognizing such language is of course part of ordinary, intersubjective exchange, as we saw earlier, involving metaphors and meanings that are shared. And the public context guides us as to when usage is figurative. (If there is doubt, clarification is sought and provided. "Did you mean that literally?" we say. Or: "I speak metaphorically . . .".) Speech occurs within a particular set of often tacit communicative rules; what Wittgenstein calls a particular "language game". And those rules almost always provide the cues we need. Within some exotic science-fiction language game, even "Someone has put thoughts into my head that are not mine" may possess something approaching a literal interpretation. But we would have to know the "local" rules specific to that game, to play it correctly. And similarly, until we understand his theology we could not even guess whether Nijinsky's claim that he is God is mere metaphor or intended more literally.[4] These may be very local rules; we are at sea without knowing them. If Nijinsky's particular "theology" is entirely unshared and idiosyncratic, moreover, we may have no way of accessing its meanings, metaphorical or otherwise.

Because of the need to understand the local context, distinguishing spiritual delusions from ordinary religious beliefs in the multicultural clinic sometimes presents problems.[5] Our concern here is conceptual, though, not clinical. Within much traditional theology, religious or spiritual belief reflects not mere metaphors, however apt, but supernatural, if ineffable, truths. Due to its theological presuppositions, such an interpretation can have only limited currency in discussions of these matters. But any such discussions can be expected to be similarly irresolvable, as there appear to be few or no agreed-upon methodological, let alone religious, assumptions within which religious delusions can be understood.

Such epistemic elusiveness suggests it would be wise to focus elsewhere than on the content of religious delusions, as has been widely recognized. Whatever makes these states delusional, it cannot usefully be seen in terms of what they are about.

SPIRITUAL DELUSIONS – EXPLANATIONS

Accounts of how religious delusions arise often employ the anomalous-experience hypotheses and two-factor theorizing described in Chapter 3 (although, what research there is, consistently blurs the important distinction between literal and more figurative "symbols," reducing its usefulness from our perspective). Much emphasis is placed on the way religious belief systems provide explanatory frameworks for what, it is hypothesized, must be alarming, unusual and untoward experiences.[6] In response to such experiences, meanings are said to be created by "collectively held symbols" (Bhavsar and Bhugra 2008: 167). And attempts to make sense of those experiences will be shaped by local frameworks, reflecting personal, family and societal meanings.[7] The role of culture is often emphasized, since spiritual delusions differ by culture in both content and frequency. (We'll return to the pervasive cultural influence of religious and spiritual ideas at the end of this chapter.) Thus, it seems to be agreed that neither the experience alone nor the beliefs alone, but some combination of these two, will explain the resulting delusional ideas.

The sources of the anomalous experiences that form part of this causal explanation are as yet little understood – as are the neural substrates of non-clinical spiritual belief and experience. Emerging agreement seems to implicate the mesolimbic system in all religious phenomenology, normal and delusional alike.[8] And neuroimaging has found an association between religious delusions and the left-temporal-lobe over-activation and left-occipital-lobe under-activity.[9] Some hypotheses implicate the particular aberrant and strange experiences thought to accompany the onset of schizophrenia, as we saw, although, since spiritual delusions occur in a number of other disorders as well, this can at best be part of the story. Moreover, here, as in the two-factor theories proposed for other delusions, the evidence that anomalous experience regularly occurs is speculative, at best.

OTHER FACTORS

Seeking to bypass the epistemic oddities of these delusional ideas, researchers have explored other ways spiritual delusions may be distinguished from more normal states of religious belief. A range of associated phenomena have been cited, some part of the social context and others idiosyncratic to the individual. Religious ideas are less likely to be categorized as delusional when there is formal religious affiliation, because of the supportive social and cognitive frameworks it provides;[10] additional signs of disorder are a clinical indicator that the belief is delusional;[11] and accompanying social dysfunction has been pointed to in assigning clinical status.[12]

As these criteria suggest, the separation between spiritual delusions and more ordinary spiritual beliefs readily admits of intermediate cases (overvalued religious ideas, for example). This seemingly large "border country" (Sims 1992, 2003) between such psychiatric phenomena and spiritual beliefs and experience was effectively demonstrated in a comparison between a group of in-patients with delusions and those from two new-age religious movements (Hare Krishnas and Druids); the study sought to determine how religious delusions differ from other religious and spiritual beliefs.[13] A control group was made up of "normal" subjects, both non-religious and religious (Christian), and beliefs were assessed in terms of their content, the distress accompanying them, the degree to which they preoccupied the subject, and the degree of conviction with which they were held. These other factors of distress, preoccupation and conviction distinguished clinical delusions, rather than their content, it was found. The subjects from new religious movements, while sharing the content of a number of delusional ideas with psychotic patients and equally convinced of their veracity, were more preoccupied or distressed by these experiences than subjects in the control group and less so than the psychotic patients.

These studies have each been focused on the part spiritual delusions play in the psychic life and behavior of the person entertaining them. The way they are acquired has received less direct research attention from those looking at spiritual delusions (although it is the subject of closely related research on the way to differentiate religious and spiritual experiences from the experiences that precede or accompany the formation of delusions).

SPIRITUAL DELUSIONS AS UNREASONABLE, UNWARRANTED

The delusion status of some beliefs is highly sensitive to cultural context and the local meanings specific to particular subgroups, as we have seen. Most definitions of delusion include the qualification that, where a belief is shared by members of a culture as part of a religious ideology, it is inaccurate to classify it as delusional. Such a "religious exception" occurs in the definition of delusion at the start of this chapter. ("The belief is not one ordinarily accepted by other members of the person's culture or subculture . . . i.e. . . . it is not an article of religious faith.")

This sort of exceptionalism, offered without explanation, has often been dismissed as unwarranted and question-begging. Idiosyncratic beliefs systems shared by only a few adherents, are likely to be regarded as delusional, it has been observed, while

> . . . belief systems which may be just as irrational but which are shared by millions are called world religions. When comparing the beliefs held by psychotics with religious beliefs held by normal people, it is impossible

to say that one set of beliefs is delusional while the other
is sane.

In defense of religious exceptionalism, however, an aspect of
the way religious and spiritual delusions are acquired has
been appealed to. Non-delusional religious beliefs often come
by way of reasons, evidence and information from authoritative sources. And although it may sometimes lead to false
beliefs, such testimony has a powerful epistemological warrant. Lacking this grounding, delusions with religious and
spiritual content have been described as "resistant to testimony" (Samuels 2009). So resistance to testimony has been
proposed as one way in which spiritual delusions such as
Nijinsky's "I am God" are distinguishable from more normal
spiritual convictions.

That we must, and are entitled to, rely on testimony in
grounding many of our beliefs is obvious and widely
accepted.[14] But philosophers disagree over the testimonial
strength of beliefs – such as theological ones – that do not
reduce to sense perception, memory and inductive inference.[15] Certainly Nijinsky's claim faces a challenge because
others deny it is true; but that may be no more than a reflection of its nature *as* unshared, and not in any way due to the
reliability of others' testimony over such contested subject
matter. The epistemic warrant provided by testimony for other
kinds of beliefs loses traction, or becomes doubtful, here.

WHEN SPIRITUAL DELUSIONS ARISE FROM DELUSIONAL
PERCEPTIONS AND SOCIAL CONTAGION

Normal religious beliefs are acquired in as many ways, probably, as there are forms of social learning. Sometimes they are

the product of methods that patently contravene our epistemic values – indoctrination and brainwashing, for example. (These are controversial categories themselves, since one person's acceptable indoctrination is another's egregious brainwashing). But more often they come through ordinary communication – emotional appeal, persuasion, teaching and, as we saw, testimony. This will likely be true of many spiritual delusions, as well, as it will delusions about themes that are, for example, ideological.

Both delusional and not, there are two ways spiritual ideas are acquired that belie this unremarkable picture. Sometimes they emerge as sudden flashes of non-inferential apprehension. And at other times, if we are to believe the historical record, these ideas are acquired through forms of social contagion. Neither way of acquiring beliefs fits with our sense of what is reasonable grounding for belief.

In *The Varieties of Religious Experience* (1961/1902), James describes mystical experiences in otherwise normal people that apparently proceed the first way. Here, the similarities to delusional perception are strikingly apparent – so much so that a non-clinical case will serve as an illustration, and reminder, of the delusional one. James quotes a (normal) young man who, on a number of occasions enjoyed, in his own words, "a period of intimate communion with the divine." These meetings came unasked and unexpected, he explains.

Once, it was when from the summit of a high mountain he looked over a vast and dramatic landscape. ". . . What I felt . . . was a temporary loss of my identity, accompanied by an illumination which revealed to me *a deeper significance than I had been wont to attach to life*" (James 1961: 71, emphasis added). Like the "delusional perception" described by MacDonald (see pp. 29–30), when the sight of faces in a passing street-car filled her with a sense of deep significance, this man's illumination occurs abruptly, without preamble; no inference links the perceptual experience to the exalted ideas it triggers.

As experiences, nothing significant appears to distinguish these two (normal and delusional) instances of intuitive apprehension. Nor of course is it experience limited to religious or spiritual content. As means of acquiring ideas, intuitive apprehension is strange and somewhat puzzling, but it is not distinctive to either delusional thought or normal religious belief.

James defends unorthodox ways of acquiring new beliefs (such as that of the young man whose account is quoted above). If they do not comply with our epistemic values, then so much the worse for those overly "rationalistic" norms, he asserts. These experiences are as convincing to those who have them as any direct sensible experiences can be, and they are ". . . much more convincing than results established by mere logic ever are." For a person who does have such experiences,

> . . . the probability is that you cannot help regarding them as genuine perceptions of truth, as revelations of a kind of reality which no adverse argument, however unanswerable by you in words, can expel from your belief. . . . If a person feels the presence of a living God . . . your critical arguments, be they never so superior, will vainly set themselves to change his faith.
>
> (James 1961: 73, 75)

Although applied to mystical religious experience, this observation has direct application to delusional perception. It seems to account for the staunch conviction with which those delusions are often maintained in the face of countervailing evidence. Describing a seemingly psychotic experience and using strikingly similar language, one patient has been quoted as saying of her intuitive apprehension: "if I'm mad, so be it, but *this is the most real thing I've ever known*" (Jackson and Fulford 1997: 47, emphasis added).

James goes on to decry the rationalistic view that all our beliefs ought ultimately to "find for themselves articulate grounds."

> . . . Vague impressions of something indefinable have no place in the rationalistic system, which on its positive side is surely a splendid intellectual tendency . . . Nevertheless . . . we have to confess that the part of [man's whole mental life] . . . will fail to convince or convert you . . . The unreasoned and immediate assurance is the deep thing in us, the reasoned argument is but a surface exhibition. Instinct leads, intelligence does but follow.
>
> (James 1961: 73–4)

Intuitions and intuitive states such as these are also valued as the source of much human creativity, and few could disagree with James that they contribute a valuable and important aspect of the whole mental life. The mathematician Gauss famously describes such an intuitive apprehension. After struggling to prove a theorem, he finally found the answer:

> . . . two days ago, I succeeded, not on account of my painful efforts but by the grace of God. Like a sudden flash of lightening, the riddle happened to be solved.
>
> (quoted in Storr 1997: 84)

Yet we can insist – as James, too, almost seems to do – that intuitive apprehensions of this kind do not comply with the epistemic norms and values that concern us here. What distinguishes intuitive apprehension from an epistemic perspective, whether in the case of spiritual experience or mathematical discovery, is its status as revealed truth, not its reasonableness or rationality.

Despite these evident similarities between creative, religious and delusional states, studies have attempted to distinguish psychotic experiences more generally from these other states, pointing to the psychic disintegration and self-absorbed nature of the former.[16] But from the vantage point of belief acquisition and epistemic norms, these contrasts leave unaffected the comparison between spiritual or creative experience and delusional perception. Whatever the advantage of intuitive thought, it does not fit into our ideas about the proper acquisition of ideas and beliefs. When it occurs with delusions of any kind it seems to partly explain their delusional nature.

Social contagion is the second source of non-rationally acquired convictions, delusional and not. Claims about the contagious spread of religious and spiritual ideas must at best be speculative. Evidence for the spread of any social contagions will by its nature be elusive, mysterious and incomplete, as we saw; we can only point towards some indirect evidence. (The extent of such effects is also debated.) Fashion trends that imperceptibly change popular taste below the level of conscious thought provide a simple illustration of how normal social behavior is the product of imitation or group contagion, we saw. Of more urgent interest than such innocent cases, however, is when social contagion results in the transmission of spiritual ideas that effect dangerous and harmful action (the case, for instance, of the religious zealot whose irrationally acquired ideas prompt violence).

Hecker's famous studies of medieval behavioral and other contagions from the 1830s (first published in English as *The Epidemics of the Middle Ages*), were introduced earlier (p. 83). He appeals to imitation (or "sympathy"; he uses the terms interchangeably), defined as "an instinct which connects individuals with the general body" (Hecker 1846: 139). Of all enthusiastic infatuations resulting from such tendencies, he observes:

> . . . that of religion is the most fertile in disorders of the mind as well as of the body, and both spread with the greatest facility by sympathy.
>
> (Hecker 1846: 142)

Hecker was closer than we are today to the religious enthusiasms of the earlier era, and he is in no doubt as to their power over the mind. He speaks of the diffusion of violent excitements, especially those of a religious or political character, which have agitated the nations of ancient and modern times, and which "may . . . pass into . . . an actual disease of the mind" (Hecker 1846: 139). His examples range far and wide, but they include the religious enthusiasm associated with Methodism and religious revivalism that spread across the United States in the first years of the nineteenth century.

Rather than emphasizing the epidemic spread of such ideas, today's research on spiritual delusions lays stress on other factors: particularly the ubiquity and pervasiveness of these ideas within contemporary cultures, and the culture-specificity of delusional content. The content of religious delusions is not simply a reflection of the patient's particular religious background or beliefs, it has been established.[17] Instead, religious symbols (or "signifiers") are "collectively held," and are "more or less readily available to the individual" (Bhavsar and Bhugra 2008: 167). Whether or not, and how, these ideas might pervade cultural awareness without being knowingly considered and adopted, can only be guessed at. Nonetheless, it seems likely that they do.

The content of spiritual delusions, we saw, makes them inaccessible to the means by which qualities such as plausibility or even truth value may be attributed to other delusional ideas. And attempts to differentiate ordinary religious and spiritual beliefs from such delusions have for the most part focused on aspects of the social context in which they are maintained, and the way they affect the rest of the person's life. We looked, instead, at aspects of how spiritual delusions have been acquired that bespeak unreasonableness, irrationality and ungroundedness. There, we saw, spiritual delusions apparently occur in the form of delusional perceptions, with the groundlessness of intuitions; and they seem likely to have been arrived at, in some cases, by social contagion.

Although these are all reasons we might attribute the status of delusions to these beliefs, none is sufficient to show them to differ from more ordinary religious and spiritual beliefs. Because of the controversy surrounding testimony as warrant for non-observational beliefs such as these, that separation cannot be achieved by appeal to the resistance to testimony marking spiritual delusions. And other epistemic features are similarly unhelpful, since many ordinary religious and spiritual beliefs seem to be acquired through comparable means – either the intuitive apprehension associated with religious experience or through social contagion. To differentiate spiritual delusions from more ordinary spiritual convictions, it seems we must rely on aspects of context or accompanying symptoms rather than of the delusions themselves.

Seven

Delusions sometimes give rise to violent action, endangering their subject and/or other people. When they have practical consequences of this kind, matters are raised that are not only epistemic but moral and social. Even the moral status of adhering to delusions when they fail to result in wrongful action deserves attention, moreover. For a fine and controversial line seems to separate some delusional states from moral weaknesses and character failings. Before examining how actions stemming from delusional thinking are assessed from a moral perspective, we'll consider this other kind of assessment, about how delusions reflect on character.

Delusions of grandeur serve as our prime example, here. First, they are extremely common. Second, embodying on-balance, and often retrospectively rebalanced, value judgements, they possess epistemic features of special philosophical complexity. And finally, they are readily understood in motivational terms. In inviting motivational analysis they are hardly alone, it is true – many common delusions do. Combining the several features just outlined, however, delusions of grandeur exhibit a moral psychology of unmatched interest.

This chapter begins with delusions of grandeur, their peculiarities and some of the implications of their transparently motivational quality. In everyday life those slightly too vain, too self-important, or too proud are as commonplace as those with the delusions of grandeur in the clinic. So, towards the end of this chapter we return to the more general issues raised by any application of motivational explanations to belief states that resemble what, outside the clinic, are recognized as – or as shading into – character weaknesses.

DELUSIONS OF GRANDEUR AS DELUSIONS OF SELF-ASSESSMENT

Delusions of grandeur fall within a grouping that includes other delusions of *self-assessment*. Of all beliefs, those not about our immediate experiences but about our selves or characters – "identity" beliefs about who we are and what we are like – seem to be some of the most prone to distortion and even delusion. And, although they have not received much attention within research on delusions during the last decades, the errors and distortions of grandiosity ("I am of the greatest imaginable importance"), narcissism ("I am enormously appealing"), and self-blame ("I am abjectly unworthy and sinful"), are commonplace in the clinic. Grandiose delusions, particularly, are associated with many diagnoses, including mania and schizophrenia; they are also allied to the non-delusional attribute of *grandiosity* found in personality disorders.

Delusions of grandeur are readily, almost inescapably, viewed in familiar motivational terms. This motivational transparency is evident in the following passage from a patient who had previously possessed an elaborate delusional system centering on his imagined identity as Jesus Christ. Of this identity, he remarks,

I liked to imagine it because I felt so useless without it . . . I
still feel inadequate now – it's as though I don't know
anything. I always felt everything I said was worthless, but as
Jesus everything I said was important – it came from God . . . I
just want to hide away, I don't feel able to cope with people . . .
I always feel lonely, I don't know what to say.

(Quoted by Roberts 1999: 172)

This passage does not indicate that the delusional ideas were willfully adopted. Nonetheless, it serves to illuminate, and perhaps explain, the satisfactions and comfort they brought this patient.

Delusions vary considerably in the ease with which they can be analyzed in motivational terms. The strange, monothematic delusions resulting from disease and damage to the brain, such as the Capgras delusion, perhaps most obviously resist such interpretation. Yet Capgras himself speculated that the patient who thinks his spouse has been replaced by an impostor is expressing a wish, or conveying ambivalence.[1] And once certain tenets of depth psychology and psychoanalysis are adopted, even the painful delusions of self-disgust and guilt associated with severe depressive states can be construed in motivational terms.

As the introduction of depth psychology suggests, much here depends on what is entailed in such a motivational account. Analyses that depict the formation of delusions as a response to unsettling and inexplicable experiences are one form of motivational analysis. The patient's distress is reduced with the formation of the delusion, on such accounts, thus the delusion can be seen as *directed to* that end. The general delusional atmosphere with all its vagueness of content must be unbearable, Jaspers remarks. So "[p]atients obviously suffer terribly under it and to reach some definite idea at last is like being relieved from some enormous burden" (Jaspers 1997: Vol. 1, 98).

More recently, explanations of the "cognitive architecture" of paranoid and depressive delusions has been analyzed by appeal to the impulse expressed in self-serving biases, as we saw earlier (p. 55).[2] Explanations ("attributions") that serve to protect the self by implicating other people when untoward events occur are offered for delusions with paranoid content. And while research suggests they are not successful in achieving their self-protective aim, that aim nonetheless can be seen as another kind of motivated response. Yet, as Tim Thornton has emphasized in a telling critique of these cognitivist analyses, such assertions apparently stretch the notion of intentionality beyond the point where it can bear a literal interpretation.[3] So the sense in which such accounts depict motivation is far from the conceptions of encoded meaning associated with reasons, as distinct from causes.

On the other hand, it is difficult to *avoid* seeing grandiose delusions as more reasoned, intentional responses. They are strikingly similar to everyday cases of motivated irrationality – a point not lost on some patients. Of his own delusions, Custance remarks:

> Of course it is all . . . pure imagination . . . I know perfectly well that in fact I have no power, that I am of no particular importance and have made rather a mess of my life. I am a very ordinary man . . . and I can truthfully say that never in the midst of the wildest flights of grandiose ideas have I ever allowed myself to forget that. Moreover, psychologically speaking, I know that my delusions of grandeur are

merely *compensation for the failures and frustrations of my* real life.

(Custance 1952: 51–2, emphasis added)

And to the similarities between grandiose delusions and everyday moral weakness and character failings is added a further complexity. Delusions of grandeur often forming part of more florid and recognizably psychotic frames of mind (within schizophrenia, for example), are also associated with the psychiatric category of personality disorder, that is located at the contested margins of disorder.

Inasmuch as they represent a kind of mirror-image to delusions of grandeur, the self-denigrating delusions associated with severe depressive states (as well as with schizophrenia), also enter our discussion. But among clinical delusions of self-assessment, delusions of grandeur most notably challenge the border between pathology and normal, if unattractive, human responses.

Nijinsky's diaries again provide our illustration. When he wrote the words below, Nijinsky *was* grand: a dance prodigy, he had made his way to principal dancer in Diaghilev's Ballets Russes, the most famous theatrical troupe in the world. So some of these claims were not entirely false.

I am the Divine savior. I am Nijinsky and not Christ. I love Christ because he was like me. I love Tolstoy because he is like me. I want to save the whole terrestrial globe from suffocation. All scientists must abandon their books and come to me. I will help everyone, for I know many things. I am a man in God. I am not afraid of death. . . . I am reason, and not intelligence. I am God, for I am reason. . . . I am the philosophy of reason. I am the true, not invented, philosophy.

(Nijinsky 1995: 225)

In another passage, he says:

> I know that if everyone feels me, God will help everyone. I see right through people. . . . My mind is so developed that I understand people without words. I see their actions and understand everything. I can do everything. I am a peasant. I am a factory worker. I am a servant. I am a gentleman. I am an aristocrat. I am a tsar. I am an Emperor. I am God. I am God. I am God. I am everything. I am life. I am eternity. I will be always and everywhere. People can kill me, but I will live because I am everything.
>
> (Nijinsky 1995: 184)

Words such as these cannot easily, if they can ever, be taken literally; and, as was observed earlier (p. 75), Nijinsky's frequent references to metaphysical qualities and status ("I am God," "I am life") leave his *Diary* as opaque as it is captivating. Nonetheless, not mere grandiosity but clinical delusions of grandeur seem to be evident in these pronouncements, and in Nijinsky's recurring theme of his supernatural, and God-like, gifts.

Due to their content, many of Nijinsky's ideas can be grouped with the spiritual delusions discussed previously, and will be heir to the problems noted in Chapter 6. Viewed *as* self-assessments, however, grandiose delusions such as these are additionally anomalous.

Clinical lore sometimes attributes delusional thinking about some facts of the matter that are true, as in the case of the delusionally jealous husband, noted earlier. Comparably, the grandiose self-assessment of the king whose status he himself attributed to divine right, might strike the denizens of modern, secular republics as like the jealous husband. The king *is* grand. But his political power, not his spiritual status, could be the sole reasonable ground for holding his (accurate) beliefs about his grandeur.

It is the balance of actual to assigned importance and value at the heart of a conception of delusional self-assessments that presents the problem here. Even setting aside cases involving a value system so idiosyncratic and unshared that it beggars understanding, the norms governing when self-assessments reflect distortion, exaggeration or misapprehension, introduce questions of proportionality made difficult in two distinct ways. They are often on-balance assessments, hard or impossible to disconfirm; and they rarely involve attributes with entirely – or widely – agreed-upon public criteria, importance or value.

As evaluative judgements, delusions of grandeur are the antithesis of delusions involving the "external reality" of traditional definitions. If to be taken literally at all, Nijinsky's confidence that he can read minds may be outright false. But even when they admit of literal meaning, most of his claims are at best implausible and far-fetched, rather than straightforwardly inaccurate. This is in part because they are often on-balance judgements, not governed by any particular, even if consensual, disconfirmation. They are also value judgements often retrospectively rebalanced and readily revised. (Such retrospective revision is not distinctive to psychopathology in any way, we all do it, frequently. For example, "We were wrong about Arthur, he was not what he appeared to be.") Finally, not only is their content relatively elusive, and inaccessible to consensual evaluation, it is also often quite "local," the way we saw the content of spiritual delusions is. It is held by a (sometimes disappearingly) small subgroup embracing those particular values or priorities.

Much of this epistemic complexity is also found with the mirror image of delusions of grandeur, delusions involving self-deprecation, and the difficulties coming from that complexity can be illustrated through them. A case example from the clinical literature describes a (depressed) man who had forgotten to give his children their pocket money and believed his sin so great that he did not deserve to live.[4] This simple case eliminates the additional difficulties inherent in on-balance self-assessments. And by any reckoning, the patient's assessment of his own wrongfulness seems disproportionate to his omission. When those who have committed real and horrible crimes are oppressed by the enormity of their sinfulness, however, finding a metric against which to judge their self-assessment will be more difficult. By the standards of their community, the assessment of their own worthlessness might be fitting.

Consider the (depressed) mother who believes she is unredeemably wicked because she has killed her children.[5] What she did may be profoundly wrong. But like the case of the king's grandiosity, or the husband's delusional jealousy, the judgement that this self-assessment is delusional will rest on the grounds or reasons involved.

The self-assessment of the patient whose terrible action was the product of further delusional beliefs (she had thought God wanted her to drown her children) may be too disturbed for us to think of blaming her. But again, unless the delusion that God wanted her to drown her children constituted her *grounds or reason for her self-assessment* – which it might be, but likely is not – then her self-assessment need not be judged delusional according to epistemic norms. As long as *the enormity of her action itself* is the reason for her self-assessment, and the proportionality it exhibits fits with consensual norms in her community or sub-community, it seems difficult to see why her self-assessment can be judged ill-grounded on that account.

The extent to which this woman's grounds or reasons for her self-assessment approach broader, on-balance, assessments will add to the epistemic difficulties raised by this case. With spiritual delusions, we saw, a comparable stalemate occurs over the reasonableness of delusions whose content, because it is not amenable to assessment in the terms of consensual reality, has to be addressed by other features of the patient's situation. And of course aspects of the context, the degree of dysfunction and suffering it brings, for example, will likely direct clinical judgement in the case of delusions of self-assessment as it will in the case of spiritual delusions. Nonetheless, if not a clinical problem, this remains a conceptual puzzle.

DELUSIONS OF SELF-ASSESSMENT AS DEFENSIVE AND MOTIVATED STATES

Within psychoanalytic thought delusions of grandeur associated with manic states are assigned to the category of *defenses*. The patient conceals from himself or represses his actual, discomforting and anxiety-provoking self-assessment by constructing (and conveying) a more positive self-image. The depth psychological account is familiar from everyday motivated irrationalities, the way we avoid and conveniently ignore unpleasant truths about ourselves, for example, and seek, and maintain, positive self-assessments. This similarity to such everyday ("self-serving") biases and to self-deception has further implications, we'll see.

The psychoanalytic account notoriously introduces intention here.[6] If we are to construe grandiose delusions as clinical states, in contrast to more everyday instances of motivated irrationality, however, we must accept that while *motivated*, the deluded patient's grandiosity is not in any straightforward way willful. (That does not preclude the subject of clinical states's having to answer to certain epistemic responsibilities, as we shall see in the chapter following this one; and clinical and everyday culpable states may still be linked by intermediate cases.)

Within the social sciences, motivated irrationality is depicted as a (statistically) normal thought pattern, and thus, while it is a bias, it is one shared by all. Self-deception, by contrast, is usually viewed as a human and universal, but moral, *failing*. (In this respect, delusions of grandeur differ from delusions of worthlessness, which are not so readily recognized in everyday psychic life. We have compassion for the person who entertains the delusional idea that his tiny infraction makes him so worthless that he does not deserve to live. His moral stature as ill, and deserving our care rather than condemnation for his harsh self-assessment is, if anything, reinforced by the inexplicability of his frame of mind.[7])

DELUSIONS OF GRANDEUR, GRANDIOSITY, AND THE SIN OF PRIDE

Perhaps the most intriguing aspect of the closeness of grandiose delusions to other motivated irrationality is the relation of clinical delusions of grandeur to the moral condemnation of those self-assessments whose inaccuracy rests in overvaluing of oneself or one's importance. That is, the vice, or sin, of pride – that "mother and Queen of all vices" so abhorred in Western religious traditions. Understood as a moral failing, pride has a characteristic that builds further parallels to clinical grandiosity, moreover. It is depicted as the weakness *most difficult to discern in ourselves* and, even when it is drawn to our attention, *hardest to acknowledge and overcome.* It "blinds Man's erring judgement and misguides the mind," as Alexander Pope says.[8]

What then is the relationship between the moral failure of pride and the grandiosity found in the clinic? Its attitude of self-love is similar, so is this blindness that makes it both hard to acknowledge and tenaciously resistant to alteration in light of outside correction.

Delusions of grandeur seem to move by imperceptible steps toward (less severe, and clinically insignificant) prideful self-love. Mid way along this apparently unmarked progression is the non-delusional trait of *grandiosity* said to distinguish (and indeed almost to comprise) the condition known as narcissistic personality disorder. Grandiosity represents middle ground. Whether it should be seen to fall on the side of *pathology* or *moral weakness*, however, is a matter of some dispute, as we shall see. And rather than aiding any attempt to distinguish between these delusions of grandeur and everyday arrogance and pridefulness, the trait of grandiosity hovers unhelpfully between them. This problem was once well-recognized within psychiatric lore, where the term "neurosis" was used of maladaptive traits that were not as severe as psychotic conditions. (Interestingly, it was then said of most neuroses that they were "mixed with the sin of pride"; Allport 1943: 735–6.)

It might be argued that our two core cases of grandiosity – those of the clinic and the confessional, as it were – must satisfy our yearning for precision here. After all, some boundaries *are* fuzzy rather than sharp, and there will always be irresolvable intermediate cases. But this response will not do here. Not only are clinical conditions and moral weakenesses different sorts of category – and as distinguishable as oil and water. In addition, the line separating the intermediate case of non-delusional grandiosity associated with personality disorder from both grandiose delusions and moral weaknesses is also alarmingly unsteady, because personality disorders themselves reside at the contested margin of mental disorder.

The status of grandiosity as a symptom of personality disorders is problematic on several counts. The inclusion of maladaptive personality traits in the broader taxonomy of mental disorders has been the subject of candid and relentless concern since the 1980s. In contrast to disorders that can be seen to involve a disease process running an identifiable course through time, personality disorders are long-term and unchanging "traits": maladaptive, inflexible patterns of perceiving, relating to, and thinking about the environment and oneself, exhibited in a wide range of social and personal contexts.[9] The conceptual difficulties that arise with counting personality disorders as mental disorders of any kind are legion. Empirical studies have cast doubt on whether the categorical model applies to personality disorders, and alternative, dimensional systems, employed to understand normal personality variation, have long been endorsed for them.[10] Such analyses and controversy cast into doubt the whole status of grandiosity as a symptom of the several personality disorders with which it is associated.

Another issue has been raised in recent research. Within the several types of personality disorder found in psychiatric classifications, a subgroup has been singled out and explicitly judged to represent *moral rather than medical* conditions.

The treatment employed for disorders in the category including narcissistic personality disorders (the Cluster B disorders, comprising antisocial, borderline, histrionic and narcissistic personality disorders), Louis Charland observes, requires a commitment to change that is typically absent in consent to therapy for other sorts of mental and behavioral disorders. With this group of personality disorders,

> [t]he central issue is whether there exists a *moral willingness* to change together with a sustained readiness to make the *moral effort* to make and sustain that change. Thus it is impossible to imagine a successful "treatment" or "cure" for these conditions that does not involve some sort of conversion or change in *moral character* . . . these are fundamental moral conditions and, consequently . . . their treatment requires a sort of *moral treatment*.
>
> (Charland 2004: 71)

If this account is right, then rather than closer to clinical grandiose delusions, the trait of grandiosity is closer to the moral failing of sinful self-love and pride.[11]

Much of the discourse of modern-day cognitive psychology is conceptually interchangeable with that of philosophy. Yet when delusions appear to be akin to more ordinary motivated irrationality, drift becomes discernible, separating and bifurcating these two disciplinary frameworks. Psychology acknowledges divergence from statistical norms in its talk of the extreme reasoning biases apparently embodied in delusional thinking. But moral and philosophical frames employ more evaluative categories, and distinguish intentional from non-intentional explanations. Between florid and insightless delusions of grandeur such as Nijinsky's, and unwarranted narcissistic self-love, self-importance and pride, lies a moral line. On which side of that line these states fall will depend on how much we can expect of the patient with respect to her epistemic capabilities and responsibilities, and how much – if not willful – her delusions nonetheless are acquired or maintained through a certain kind of negligence. Since some of the same responsibilities are called for in the case introduced in the chapter that follows, of action taken out of delusions, that discussion may be deferred.

Eight

Both holding, and acting on, delusions sometimes call for moral assessment, and those assessments are the subject of this chapter.

When dangerous deeds such as those of the violent maniac and the religious or ideological zealot result from delusional states, how are they to be evaluated? *Delusional agency*, when a person acts out of, or upon, delusional ideas, has often been judged to be broadly exculpating, and exculpating *simpliciter*. Yet the range and variety found among clinical delusions suggest a more nuanced picture. Delusional agency often exculpates. It admits of assessment as culpable when a range of conditions apply, however, conditions involving belief states, reasoning capabilities, degree of insight, and measure of self-control. Two implications of this complexity are stressed here: that such assessment will remain unchanged whether we adopt a continuum or categorical view of delusions, and that the same considerations affecting how we hold and act on ordinary beliefs guide assessments about how we hold and act on delusional states.

The categorical view of abnormal mental states comfortably accommodates moral and social attitudes that are widely accepted and agreed upon. If we believe delusions stem from identifiable dysfunction that interferes with a person's autonomous action, we are inclined to set aside blame and adopt attitudes of sympathy and compassion towards the sufferer. This is conspicuously so in the case of delusional agency. She who harms another because of the delusional misapprehension that her own life is threatened, we suppose, represents a particularly powerful kind of exception to our usual moral intuitions about the blameworthiness of inflicting harm on others. And if delusions are seen to direct the action of those who are violent and disordered, it is customary to withhold blame in the legal as well as everyday spheres, affording protection from punishment through the insanity defense and the other legal structures supporting it.

Widely recognized, this much has received explication within jurisprudence and moral philosophy. The moral responses where blame and condemnation are replaced by forgiveness and an impulse to help might at first seem less suited to analyses that place disorder and delusion on a continuum with normal states. To maintain the separation between culpability for which blame is appropriate, and exculpating delusional agency, a conventional, and arguably arbitrary, line must be drawn. So it must to offer support and sympathy rather than condemnation for the person whose overblown self-assessments are understood to be symptoms of mental disorder, as we saw in the last chapter. It is the conventional nature of this moral distinction that seems at first sight difficult to accommodate with our moral intuitions about blame and culpability. Whether we regard delusions as different in kind or degree from more normal states, however, the multidimensional aspect of delusions and their complex epistemic normativity allows us to evaluate delusional agency recognizing the same excusing conditions and qualifications we employ when we assess violent and destructive actions borne of more normal states. Delusions sometimes *compel* action; then, the action must be excused, just as it is when, as occasionally happens, anyone is compelled to act. And when there is a lack of insight extreme enough to prevent the person from recognizing, let alone adhering to, her epistemic responsibilities, she will similarly be excused. But certain sorts of ignorance also alter our moral judgements in both personal and legal assessments of ordinary agency. Although ignorance can be culpable, it is not always. We often forgive the failings of the person who does not know what she does; within the criminal law, similarly, some forms of ignorance serve as excuses. So this, too, is an aspect of our usual moral attitudes that applies to actions resulting from delusions.

DELUSIONAL AGENCY

The rather sparse empirical research addressing those whose violent and harmful actions stem from their delusions has yielded a number of findings, and these are both negative, and somewhat unexpected. Delusional action does not correlate with delusions showing greater conviction, preoccupation, systematization or insightlessness.[1] Instead, at least as patients themselves understood what occurred, those with seemingly greater epistemic capabilities, who sought out evidence to confirm or refute their delusional belief, and seemed to be willing to countenance the hypothetical contradiction of those beliefs, were more inclined to act on them. (Perhaps less surprisingly, they also reported feeling sad, frightened or anxious as a consequence of the delusion, so their distress, rather than their epistemic capabilities, may be the determining factor in their having chosen to take action.) Since such relatively unimpaired epistemic capabilities have also been correlated with a greater likelihood of recovery, we may at least set aside the presumption that clinical severity augurs delusional, harmful action.

There is surely something right about our impulse to withhold blame when delusions direct violent action this way. Self-control cannot be expected of, nor full responsibility attributed to, those gripped by the distortion and goading of dangerously antisocial and self-critical delusions. But if we adopt a continuum view of delusions, we must understand when, and how, delusions could excuse. This requires us to reflect on the provenance, degree, severity and compelling power of those delusions that drive violent action.

First, even if (as those empirical studies suggest) lack of insight is not correlated with delusional action, the presence or absence of insight marks an important philosophical divide. The "seasoned" patient, with a better understanding of herself, stands in contrast to the one who (unaware that her delusions may not be real, or shared, for example) lacks all insight into her condition. The delusional agency of the person aware but neglectful of certain epistemic responsibilities may be culpable in ways that the delusional agency of the person unaware of the flaws in his thinking cannot be.

John Perceval's *Narrative*, introduced earlier (Chapter 4), in which he recounts his year in a private madhouse and the "natural but often erroneous . . . confused judgement" he experienced, again offers acute observation on this point. There is a power in man, Perceval explains,

> which independent of his natural thought and will, can form ideas upon his imagination – control his voice – and even wield his limbs. Only when a person *recognizes that he* can resist the power from this source, recovery comes from this condition.

To illustrate, Perceval describes a particular occasion when, instead of giving in to the power directing his voice to utter obscenities, he "chose to be silent, rather than obey." Thus, he says, he was "cured of the folly that I was to yield my voice up to the control of any spirit . . . without discrimination," and so his mind came to be

> set at rest in great measure from another delusion; or rather, the superstitious belief that I was blindly to yield myself up to an extraordinary guidance was done away.
>
> (Quoted in Kaplan 1964: 252–3)

Depicting this struggle to wrest control of his voice and limbs from the unconscious power that has directed them, Perceval's "without *discrimination*" and "*blindly* to yield myself" indicate the epistemic nature of the effort involved. By applying the means usually employed to evaluate the good sense of our impulses and plausibility of our beliefs ("discriminate" is his word), rather than blindly bypassing that exercise, he suggests, he was able to regain control.

Whether the return of Perceval's reason resulted from this struggle we will never know. But certainly his description matches other accounts of this kind of epistemic exercise. Closer to our era, John Nash has spoken of his efforts to distinguish hallucinated from real experience, and delusional from warranted belief. He learned, he says, to "discriminate" and reject the paranoid ideas and attitudes to which he had been prey earlier in his life, when he was beset by dangerous, alarming and debilitating psychotic episodes. Looking back, he has remarked that gradually he began

> to intellectually reject some of the delusionally-influenced lines of thinking which had been characteristic of my

orientation. This began, most recognizably, with the rejection
of politically-oriented thinking as essentially a hopeless
waste of intellectual effort.

Nash analogizes this effort of will to the role of willpower
in other spheres: "if one *makes an effort* to 'rationalize' one's
thinking" he concludes,

> then one can simply recognize and reject the irrational
> hypotheses of delusional thinking.
> > (Both passages are quoted in Nash's biography,
> > Nasar 1998: 353, 356, emphasis added)

The Center Cannot Hold (2007), Elyn Saks's memoir of her
experiences with schizophrenia, depicts similar epistemic
efforts. Knowing to conceal her delusions, she speaks of working "to keep my symptoms out of view from . . . friends" (Saks
2007: 287). Even when in the thrall of those delusions, she
recognized that to talk about her recurrent delusion of killing
children or being able to destroy cities with her mind "was
not part of polite conversation"; she was just enough in the
real world, as she puts it,

> to know that what I was thinking much of the time wasn't
> real – *or at least it wouldn't be real to* [her friend; Sam.
> > (Saks 2007: 99, emphasis added)

Although her description is not cast in such terms, we may
suppose that only something close to Nash's epistemic efforts
could have permitted Saks to *know her delusions would not be real
to Sam.*

The discriminating efforts described by Nash have some
parallels in everyday experience. (They are also found in cognitive therapy, where patients are encouraged to engage in

systematic assessments of the grounds for their delusional beliefs, we saw [p. 63].) If we were ideally rational, we would subject all our "irrational hypotheses" to such scrutiny, and we fall considerably short of this ideal, undoubtedly. Yet there are differences between the self-conscious epistemic exercise Nash describes, and the habits of even the most flawed of normal reasoners: much of the intersubjective verification that allows us to assess our impulses and belief states this way is habituated – tacit, and effortless. (Employing the language sometimes applied to these epistemic capabilities, we can say that like all effective virtues, they have long since become habits.)

This is an advantage enjoyed by normal reasoners and sometimes lost to those plagued by delusional ideas. However, neither it, nor its loss, is initially recognized by the subjects of those ideas. The first experience of hallucinations and delusions, it seems apparent, will find their subject as unaware of the need for such extra efforts *as most people are*. Only with caution born of past episodes of these states can come recognition of the necessity for any process of self-conscious monitoring.

So moral as well as epistemic differences separate the naive recipient of delusions from the seasoned and insightful one. Once the unreliability of his judgements has been recognized, some small measure of self-control sometimes lies within reach, as it did in Nash's case. And with that self-control and awareness come responsibilities.

The presence of severe disorder often, and rightly, serves to limit the demands imposed upon its sufferer. And responsibility, of course, admits of degree. Nonetheless, some responsibilities are expected of the person whose condition endangers or inconveniences themselves or others. (Following medical regimes as prescribed is an example of one of these.) And in a similar way, the seasoned delusional person would seem to be encumbered with responsibilities that are epistemic in focus, but also moral: checking and verifying judgements and what might be faulty impressions, in something like the way Nash describes. When his delusions are part of his practical life, the person who knows *he is generally prone to delusion* would seem reasonably expected to show this extra epistemic care.

How realistic are these demands? The person whose actions arise from delusion, according to clinical lore, will likely continue to lack insight into his condition even after having been made aware of it. And such a deficit must prevent compliance with the sort of epistemic responsibilities sketched, even in a less naive subject. This account, where the patient knows but cannot accept the delusional status of his beliefs will be apt in some cases, undeniably. But the presumption that delusional thinking is always accompanied by impaired insight – a mainstay of psychiatric wisdom during the second half of the twentieth century – has recently been questioned. Only 60 to 70 percent of patients with severe disorder have been judged to have some impairment of their capacity for insight, newer studies suggest.[2] And the lack of insight associated with psychosis is now recognized to be a matter of degree and to involve several dimensions. It comprises an assortment of beliefs (about one's disorder) variously present and absent in the patient with delusions.[3]

The central treatment goal of enhancing the patient's insight into the illness recognizes the epistemic imperative outlined above. Although a greater degree of insight on the patient's part is correlated with a more hopeful prognosis, achieving insight is not an end in itself. But if he is entirely lacking insight into his plight, the psychotic patient cannot be expected to recognize the need for these small ways of gaining control over his cognitive states. (In light of recent studies critical of the overly medical language of the demand for insight, it should be pointed out that these formulations can and perhaps should be framed in non-medical terms.[4])

The effects of delusion on reasoning are sometimes narrowly circumscribed, and the limited scope of the apparent reasoning bias involved in some delusions, we saw, has puzzled researchers. It has been noted as a feature distinguishing delusional from more normal, and more integrated, frames of mind. But the isolation or compartmentalization of some delusional beliefs perhaps reflects an epistemic advantage here. Its epistemic status may be obscured by lack of insight, still the *general* belief ("I am prone to delusional thinking") or general epistemic prescription ("Check with someone else about judgements concerning my superior talents") may not have been affected.

Arguably, some formulations required by the demand for insight, such as "I am presently psychotic," cannot be prescribed as any kind of epistemic duty because they express a self-referential paradox.[5] But that allows for mental exercises involving less paradoxical thoughts: "Because I have sometimes been psychotic, I must always check with someone else before making generalizations about my own talents," for example, or "Because I have sometimes been psychotic, I should seek treatment."

Depictions of the dangerous patient succumbing to an irresistibly strong impulse to act seem to point to another reason the person subject to delusional agency may be incapable of undertaking epistemic exercises such as these. That this is an accurate account in some cases is undeniable. Writing of commands that came to her as "shapeless, powerful beings that controlled me with thoughts (not voices) that had been placed in my head" Saks depicts a state of powerlessness: "It never occurred to me that disobedience was an option . . . I *do not make the rules, I just follow them.*" When another "thought or message" was to hurt herself, she says,

> [t]o inflict pain on myself because that was what I was worthy of . . . I burned myself – with cigarettes, lighters . . . electric heaters, boiling water.
>
> (Saks 2007: 85)

The degree to which, as Saks says, disobedience is not an option, will vary during the course of the patient's condition, our memoirs also show. The transition from self-control to an irresistible impulse to self harm is described in *Diary of a Schizophrenic Girl*. At first, there was great suffering:

> . . . It seemed that my mouth was full of birds which I crunched between my teeth, and their feathers, their blood and broken bones were choking me. . . .

In the midst of this horror, Renee continues, she nonetheless carried on her work as a secretary – until, one day,

> The orders became more imperious, more demanding . . . When I understood the mechanism of the System of Punishments which engulfed me, I fought less and less against the orders . . . One day, trembling, I placed the back of my right hand on the incandescent coals and held it there as long as possible. . . .
>
> (Sechehaye 1994: 59–60)

Renee at first was able to keep her impulses in check. Later, she was not. Far from blaming Renee for succumbing to these inner demands, we recognize as valiant her struggle to resist their goading. Sometimes, we also recognize, people *are* compelled to act on impulses that are well-nigh irresistible. Phenomenological and clinical reports of the sequence of withstanding and then succumbing to inner imperatives suggest, however, that delusional agency exhibits *all the range and variety of normal agency* in this respect. Some patients describe actions as intensely compelled as Renee's eventually were. At other times long planning, and a thoughtful, even ruminative, assessment of means and ends are depicted; at others still, action seems haphazard, almost aimless.

If this diverse set of factors and contexts can be summed up, it must be with extensive qualifications. Delusional agency may admit of assessment as culpable, we can conclude, but only when a range of conditions are met: when it is accompanied by a general belief that is insightful ("I am prone to delusional thinking"); when reasoning out of that general belief remains unimpaired; when, in the "seasoned" patient, epistemic responsibilities have been neglected; and when the intensity of the impulse to act does not eclipse all else.

Normal agency exhibits variation along each of these dimensions, even the last. And if it is known to stem from intensely felt attitudes or undeniable bias, ordinary motivation is sometimes assessed with similar caution, and some more ordinary actions are experienced as irresistibly compelled, and beyond self-control. If delusions or delusion-like ideas are the result of strangely acquired, ill-grounded, ideas, maintained without adequate reasons, and they are the goad for violent action, we can suppose each of the moral considerations outlined above will apply. The material and more obvious harm brought about by such actions, whether delusional or not, must strike us most immediately. Nonetheless, some fuller reckoning invites itself. To the moral wrongfulness of the harm those actions bring about must be added the wrongful neglect of epistemic responsibilities.

Whether we adopt a continuum or a categorical model of clinical delusions, the same dimensions occur and moral distinctions apply. And they differ in no significant way from the considerations affecting how we view normal agency when it results in harmful action. Rather than in any general way serving to excuse, actions taken on or from delusional thinking are still to be assessed morally the way other, more ordinary, actions are.

Afterword

The broader societal implications of the set of ideas introduced in the preceding pages were not drawn out. They are considerable, nonetheless, and of quite urgent significance.

The last decades of the twentieth century, and the first decade of the present one, have been jarring in any number of respects – philosophical, certainly, but also social and political. In particular, we have seen psychopathology that, through the Internet and other technological means, seems to spread with the speed and mindlessness of epidemics. And we have witnessed the prominence of violence in the name of religious and ideological ideas, reminiscent of nothing so much as the contagious religious "enthusiasms" of earlier times. This book does no more than signal some of these links: the category of delusions, so central to our modernist philosophical traditions (and now the subject of a belated interest among philosophers and cognitive psychologists); its seeming shading off into delusion-like states and from thence into more ordinary errors; its unresolved status in relation to the beliefs underlying group behavioral pathologies; its uncomfortable fit with religious and ideological ideas; its history in the madness of crowds, and tie to social contagions that have become exponentially more potent in our viral times.

Notes

INTRODUCTION

1 *Leviathan* Ch. 8, p. 141.
2 M. Jackson 2007.
3 Storr 1997, Munro 1999.
4 This sort of normative rationality is sometimes said to be epistemic, in contrast to procedural (Bayne and Fernández 2008).
5 See Bentall 2003, for example.
6 Interestingly, the first decade of the twenty-first century has also seen claims like those sketched here about delusional states in the experiential surround of auditory hallucinations. Many sources attest to the prevalence of inner voices that are frequently benign, and even a source of comfort for their subjects.
7 Preface, p. xx of the 1852 edn; see Mackay 1993: xvii.
8 For the considerable diagnostic agreement among those identifying delusions, see Bell et al. 2006 and Munro 1999: 34–5.
9 Much of this research has been in the pages of *Philosophy, Psychiatry & Psychology*, and *Mind & Language*. Important edited collections include Coltheart and Davies 2000, Chung et al. 2007, Bayne and Fernández 2008 and Broome and Bortolotti 2009.
10 See Radden 2008.
11 Jaspers 1997a: Vol. 1, 55.

ONE   DELUSIONS AND CULTURAL MEANING

1 In his far-reaching analysis of the role of these passages from the *Meditations* in the history of madness, Foucault goes further, concluding that here we see madness "quashed by the exercise of Reason" a new

sovereign that "rules a domain where the only possible enemies are errors and illusions" (Foucault 2006: 44, 46).

2   In eighteenth-century aesthetic ideas, including Kant's, *sensus communis* took on the related but more specific meaning of shared taste.

3   The theory Schopenhauer constructed on the basis of these observations resembles those later expounded by Freud to a quite striking degree: mental disorder involved memory lapses due to the expunging of traumatic experiences that have been papered over with false memories.

4   See Foucault 1961; Derrida 1978; Gilman 1985; Thiher 2002; Felman 1975 – for example.

5   For the link to *logos*, see Thiher 2002.

TWO   VARIETIES OF CLINICAL DELUSION

1   Sacks et al. 1974.

2   See, for example, Musalek 2003; Sass and Parnass 2001.

3   Kraepelin's separation of these into distinct disorders has been defended against their subsumption into the category of schizophrenia, for example (see Munro 1999).

4   Fulton and Bailey 1929.

5   Hirstein 2005: 177.

6   This analysis is from Hirstein 2005.

7   Hirstein 2005: 3–4.

8   This ability to critically evaluate a perceptual experience has been described as the inhibition of a pre-potent doxastic response (Davies et al. 2001: 149).

9   Sims 2003: 123.

10   Karimi et al. 2007.

11   Heidegger 1962.

12   This has been variously described. Wernicke (1900) introduced the concept of an *autochthonous idea*, one that was aboriginal and arising without external cause. Writing in 1911, Bleuler speaks of delusional ideas that enter consciousness already complete without having been precipitated by hallucinations, and which patients cannot trace to their origins, as "primordial" delusions (Bleuler 1950: 384).

13   Jaspers 1997.

14   Kempf et al. 2005.

15 See Tsuang et al. 2007; Kempf et al. 2005.

16 See Pillay et al. 1998.

17 For a fuller account of this condition, see Munro 1999: 201–8.

18 Introduced into French psychiatry during the nineteenth century, the category has been labeled many ways ("induced insanity," "psychosis of association," "communicated insanity," "reciprocal insanity," "symbiotic association" and more).

19 This case is from Kim et al. 2003: 462–3.

20 Earlier classifications had introduced the idée fixe or überwertige Idée, and these were antecedents.

21 Veale 2002.

22 McKenna 1984.

THREE   RESEARCH CONTROVERSIES

1 See Ellis and Young 1990; Ellis et al. 1997.

2 See Kendler and Gardner 1998.

3 The examples are from Samuels 2009.

4 This is a "homeostatic property cluster" model, comprising members sharing non-accidentally related, although logically unrelated, properties (Samuels 2009: 13). He sketches the kind of natural kind they could be, multiply realizable, generic, cognitive kinds whose members characteristically exhibit those properties enumerated in standard accounts of delusion.

5 Samuels 2009: 40–1.

6 Murphy 2006.

7 It will in this respect be no different from much other science (Murphy 2006).

8 A thorough discussion of the implications and plausibility of the doxastic position is to be found in Lisa Bortolotti's *Delusions and Other Irrational Beliefs* (2010).

9 Berrios 1991.

10 When they seem inappropriately elated or discouraged, we perhaps can attribute delusional feeling states to others. (I am grateful to Amélie Rorty for this example.)

11 See Currie 2000.

12 Bayne and Pacherie 2005.

13 Ibid. 2005.

14 Hamilton 2007.

15 Hurlburt 1990, 1993; Hurlburt and Schwitzgebel 2007.

16 This has been proposed by Frankish. Beliefs are taken to be conscious states yet sometimes we seem to understand them to be non-conscious states; in some, but not all, contexts they are treated as under conscious control; sometimes they are represented as all or nothing (I believe it or I do not), while at other times as probabilistic and hedged. These tensions, Frankish surmises, reflect beliefs understood as discrete states of a cognitive system that can be selectively activated in reasoning; or as holistically interdependent, multi-track behavioral dispositions (Frankish 2009: 272–6).

17 See Von Domarus 1944.

18 Kempf et al. 2005; Bentall and Young 1996.

19 Maher 1988.

20 This study is described in Fine 2006.

21 Davies et al. 2001: 149.

22 Garety and Hemsley 1994.

23 Rhodes and Gipps 2008.

24 McLaughlin 2008.

25 Frith 1992.

26 See Davies et al. 2001.

FOUR   DO DELUSIONS MEAN ANYTHING?

1 See Tirrell 1993; Langton 1993; Potter 2000.

2 For recognition of this, see Roberts 1999: 155–6.

3 See Bolton and Hill 1996.

4 Phillips 1996.

5 This may not be a sharp distinction, for no adequate account separates bizarre from non-bizarre delusions (Heinimaa 2003).

6 See Kingdon and Turkington 1994; Chadwick et al. 1996.

7 See Smith 2007; Leudar and Thomas 2001.

8 Other memoirists decry the attribution of meaningfulness to psychotic experience, it should be added. Susannah Kaysen speaks of her disordered thoughts as "*synthetic, and without meaning* . . . idiot mantras that exist in a prearranged cycle. . . ." Once, these thoughts must have "meant what they said" . . . but repetition has blunted them. They have

become background music, a Muzak medley of self-hatred themes (Kaysen 1993: 78).

9 The example comes from Dancy 1985: 107–8.

10 Gillett 1994.

11 For a recent critique of the "bedrock" theory, see forthcoming work by Bortolotti, "Shaking the Bedrock."

12 Cutting and Murphy 1990; de Bonis et al. 1997.

13 Claims like Perceval's have also been put forward by more recent theorists. (See Kraus 2007, for example.)

14 These rules are looser, granted: in philosophical writing, metaphor is said to be rule-*influenced* rather than rule-*governed* (Soskice 1985; Kittay 1987).

15 Stiver 1996.

16 Metaphor can be defined as the mapping of ideas from one conceptual domain to another. Closely related and also seemingly disturbed in delusional thought is metonymy, when one aspect of a conceptual domain stands for another aspect in the same domain.

17 Black 1954–5; Lakoff and Johnson 1980.

18 Laing's position here contrasts with that of Jaspers. In resisting the possibility that primary delusions might have meaning, Jaspers criticized thinkers such as Jung (and Freud), disparaging the interpretation of all apparently incomprehensible phenomena, including dreams, as wish-fulfillment.

19 Interestingly, Sass has also posited that a form of motivated, obfuscating language characterizes schizophrenia and claimed that the schizophrenic has special reason to resort to metaphors of a reified and mechanistic kind (Sass 1994). Similarly, Kraus explains the frequency of delusional themes that are mechanistic as an attempt to convey the strangeness of the experiences resulting from delusional moods in schizophrenia (Kraus 2007).

FIVE   DELUSIONS AS SHARED: *FOLIES À DEUX* AND THE MADNESS OF CROWDS

1 Munro 1999.

2 See Shiwach and Sobin 1998, and for a challenge, Lazarus 1986.

3 Kim et al. 2003.

4 For a discussion of these and further categories, see Shimizu et al. 2007.

5 Alongside the individualistic features of the disciplines studying and treating clinical delusions that separate endogenous from such exogenous states may be added Jaspers's dismissal. Most group delusions are relegated to the status of "illusions," he asserts. Only mass beliefs that "reach the highest ranks of absurdity" deserve the term delusion. A belief in witches, is his example – and even that, he adds, need not be a delusion "in the psychopathological sense" (Jaspers 1997: Vol. 1, 104).

6 That not all these epidemics had psychogenic origins is suggested by compelling historical evidence implicating the part played by ergot poisoning (Matossian 1989).

7 For more recent research on the involuntary effect of imitation and suggestibility see Schumaker 1991.

8 Sargant 1957; Lifton 1969.

9 See Hurley and Chater 2005; Meltzoff and Prinz 2002; Gallese 2002.

10 See Eysenck 1991.

11 Phillips et al. 1995; Munro 1999.

12 Cororve and Gleaves 2001.

13 See Schumaker 1991.

14 Hesse-Biber 2007: 2–3.

15 For the prevalence of eating disorders, postulated to affect about 15 percent of high-school and college females, see Hsu 1996.

16 For the combination of unshared individual risk factors and shared influences that bring about binge-eating behavior, see Crandell 2004, for example.

17 See Schumaker 1991.

18 See Harré and Tissaw 2005: 80–1.

19 A welcome new analysis of the issues introduced in this chapter is in Laurie Reznek's Delusions and the Madness of the Masses (in press).

SIX SPIRITUAL DELUSIONS – RELIGIOUS, METAPHYSICAL, IDEOLOGICAL

1 By one measure, 24 percent of a large sample of hospitalized patients exhibited religious delusions (Drinnan and Lavender 2006: 318); on another estimate 25 to 39 percent of patients with schizophrenia, and

15 to 22 percent of those with bipolar disorder, have religious delusions (Koenig 2009: 286).

2 DSM-IV-TR (*Diagnostic and Statistical Manual of Mental Disorders*, 4 edn, text revised), see APA 2000.

3 These examples are Spitzer's (1990).

4 Adding to the complexity here, some "non-realist" thinkers deny that theological claims such as those about God can have literal meaning (Stiver 1996: 131).

5 Ng 2007: 63.

6 Pargament 1997; Drinnan and Lavender 2006.

7 Ng 2007: 64.

8 Saver and Rabin 1997; Ng 2007.

9 Puri et al. 2001.

10 Koenig 2009.

11 Sims 1992.

12 Jackson and Fulford 1997: 55.

13 Peters et al. 1999.

14 Coady 1992.

15 Lackey and Sosa 2006.

16 Chadwick 2001; Brett 2002.

17 Corin et al. 2004; Siddle et al. 2004.

SEVEN DELUSIONS AS VICES

1 Capgras and Carette 1924.

2 See Bentall 2003; Garety and Freeman 1999.

3 See Thornton 2007: 154–9.

4 Fulford 1991: 108.

5 This is loosely based on the 2001 case of Andrea Yates.

6 Sartre 1956.

7 To explain such paradoxical attitudes, psychoanalytic theories have been required to develop a series of depth-psychological tenets, many of them heirs to Freud's ideas in his great essay on mourning and melancholia, in which the split psyche turns upon part of itself; others have employed the idea of internalized societal attitudes to explain such self-critical assessments.

8 "Of all the causes which conspire to blind Man's erring judgement, and misguide the mind, / What the weak head with strongest bias

rules, / Is pride, the never-failing vice of fools." Alexander Pope, *An Essay on Criticism* (1711).

9 This is taken from APA 1994: 630.
10 See Livesley 1998.
11 For an attempt to challenge Charland's analysis, see Pitkin 2009.

EIGHT   DELUSIONS AND VIOLENCE

1 Buchanan et al. 1993.
2 Ghaemi 2003: 232.
3 David 1990; Amador and David 1998.
4 Reimer forthcoming.
5 See Reimer forthcoming; Radden forthcoming.
6 For a recent case discussion of the issues raised in this chapter see Broome, Bortolotti and Mameli (2010).

Bibliography

Allport, G. (1943) Review of *The Psychology of Character* by Rudolph Allers, *American Sociological Review* 8, no. 6: 735–6.

Amador, X. and David, A. (eds) (1998) *Insight and Psychosis*, Oxford: Oxford University Press.

APA (American Psychiatric Association) (1994) *Diagnostic and Statistical Manual of Mental Disorders*, 4 edn (DSM-IV), Washington, DC: American Psychiatric Press.

—— (2000) *Diagnostic and Statistical Manual of Mental Disorders*, 4 edn, text revised (DSM-IV-TR), Washington, DC: American Psychiatric Press.

Arnone, D., Patel, A. and Tan, G. (2006) "The Nosological Significance of Folie à Deux: A Review of the Literature," *Annals of General Psychiatry* 5: 1–8.

Bayne, T. and Fernández, J. (eds) (2008) *Delusion and Self-Deception: Affective and Motivational Influences on Belief Formation*, New York: Psychology Press.

Bayne, T. and Pacherie, E. (2005) "In Defence of the Doxastic Conception of Delusions," *Mind & Language* 20, no. 2: 163–88.

Bell, V. Halligan, P. W. and Ellis, H. D. (2006) "Diagnosing Delusions: A Review of Inter-rater Reliability," *Schizophrenia Research* 86, nos 1–3: 76–9.

Bentall, R. P. (1990). "The Illusion of Reality: A Review and Integration of Psychological Research on Hallucinations," *Psychological Bulletin* 107, no. 1: 82–95.

—— (2003) *Madness Explained: Psychosis and Human Nature*, London: Penguin.

Bentall, R. P. and Young, H. F. (1996) "Sensible Hypothesis Testing in Deluded, Depressed and Normal Subjects," *British Journal of Psychiatry* 163: 372–5.

Berrios, G. (1991) "Delusion as 'wrong beliefs': A Conceptual History," *British Journal of Psychiatry* 159 (suppl. 14): 6–13.

Bhavsar, V. and Bhugra, D. (2008) "Religious Delusions: Finding Meaning in Psychosis," *Psychopathology* 41, no. 3: 165–72.

Black, M. (1954–55) "Metaphor," *Proceedings of the Aristotelian Society*, n.s. 55: 273–94.

Bleuler, E. (1950) *Dementia Praecox or the Group of Schizophrenias*, trans. Joseph Zinkin, New York: International Universities Press.

Bolton, D. and Hill, C. (1996) *Mind, Meaning and Mental Disorder: The Nature of Causal Explanation in Psychology and Psychiatry*, Oxford: Oxford University Press.

Bortolotti, L. (2010) *Delusions and Other Irrational Beliefs*, Oxford: Oxford University Press.

—— (Forthcoming) "Shaking the Bedrock," *Philosophy, Psychiatry & Psychology*.

Bracken, P. and Thomas, P. (2005) *Postpsychiatry: Mental Health in a Postmodern World*, Oxford: Oxford University Press.

Brett, C. (2002) "Psychotic and Mystical States of Being: Connections and Distinctions," pts 1 and 2, *Philosophy, Psychiatry & Psychology* 9, no. 4: 321–41, and 11, no. 1: 35–41.

Broome, M. (2004) "The Rationality of Psychosis and Understanding the Deluded," *Philosophy, Psychiatry & Psychology* 11, no. 1: 35–41.

Broome, M. and Bortolotti, L. (eds) (2009) *Psychiatry as Cognitive Neuroscience: Philosophical Perspectives*, Oxford: Oxford University Press.

Broome, M., Bortolotti, L. and Mameli, M. (2010) "Moral Responsibility and Mental Illness: A Case Study," *Cambridge Quarterly of Healthcare Ethics* 19: 179–187.

Buchanan, A., Reed, A., Wessely, S., Garety, P., Taylor, Grubin, D. and Dunn, G. (1993) "Acting on Delusions II: The Phenomenological Correlates of Acting on Delusions," *British Journal of Psychiatry* 163: 77–81.

Campbell, J. (2001) "Rationality, Meaning, and the Analysis of Delusion," *Philosophy, Psychiatry & Psychology* 8, nos 2–3: 89–100.

Capgras, J. and Carette, P. (1924) "Illusion de sosies et complexe d'Oedipe," *Annales Medico-Psychologique* 82: 48–68.

Chadwick, P. (2001) "Sanity to Supersanity to Insanity: A Personal Journey," in I. Clarke (ed.) *Psychosis and Spirituality: Exploring the New Frontier*, London: Whurr, pp. 75–89.

Chadwick, P., Birchwood, M. and Trower, P. (1996) *Cognitive Therapy for Delusions, Voices and Paranoia*, Chichester, UK: Wiley.

Charland, L. (2004) "Character: Moral Treatment and the Personality Disorders," in J. Radden (ed.) *The Philosophy of Psychiatry: A Companion*, New York: Oxford University Press, pp. 64–77.

Chung, M., Fulford, W. and Graham, G. (eds) (2007) *Reconceiving Schizophrenia*, Oxford: Oxford University Press.

Coady, A. J. (1992) *Testimony: A Philosophical Study*, Oxford: Oxford University Press.

Coltheart, M. and Davies, M. (eds) (2000) *Pathologies of Belief*, Oxford: Blackwell.

Cooper, P. J. and Fairburn, C. G. (1984) "Confusion over the Core Psychopathology of Bulimia Nervosa," *International Journal of Eating Disorders* 13, no. 4: 385–9.

Corin, E., Thara, R. and Padmavati, R. (2004) "Living in a Staggering World: The Play of Signifiers in Early Psychosis in South India," *Cambridge Studies in Medical Anthropology* 11: 110–45.

Cororve, M. B. and Gleaves, D. H. (2001) "Body Dysmorphic Disorder," *Clinical Psychology Review* 21, no. 6: 949–70.

Crandell, C. S. (2004) "Social Contagion of Binge Eating," in R. M. Kowalski and M. R. Leary (eds) *The Interface of Social and Clinical Psychology: Key Reading*, New York: Psychology Press, pp. 99–115.

Crossley, D. (1995) "Religious Experience within Mental Illness," *British Journal of Psychiatry* 166: 284–6.

Currie, G. (2000) "Imagination, Delusion and Hallucinations," *Mind & Language* 15, no. 1: 168–83.

Custance, J. (1952) *Wisdom, Madness and Folly: The Philosophy of a Lunatic*, New York: Pellegrini & Cudahy.

Cutting, J. and Murphy, D. (1990) "Preference for Denotative as Opposed to Connotative Meanings in Schizophrenics," *Brain and Language* 39: 459–68.

Dancy, J. (1985) *Introduction to Contemporary Epistemology*, Oxford: Blackwell.

David, A. (1990) "Insight and Psychosis," *British Journal of Psychiatry* 156: 798–808.

Davies, M., Coltheart, M., Langdon, R. and Breen, N. (2001) "Monothematic Delusions: Toward a Two-Factor Account," *Philosophy, Psychiatry & Psychology* 8, no. 2–3: 133–58.

de Bonis, M., Epelbaum, C., Deffez, V. and Feline, A. (1997) "The Comprehension of Metaphors in Schizophrenia," *Psychopathology*, vol. 30, no. 3: 149–54.

Derrida, J. (1978) *Writing and Difference*, London: Routledge & Kegan Paul.

Descartes, R. (1960/1641) *Meditations on First Philosophy*, trans. L. Lafleur, New York: Bobbs Merrill.

Diethelm, O. and Heffernan, T. F. (1965) "Felix Platter and Psychiatry," *Journal of the History of Behavioral Sciences* 1: 10–23.

Dijksterhuis, A. (2005) "Why We Are Social Animals: The High Road to Imitation as Social Clue," in S. Hurley and N. Chater (eds) *Perspectives on Imitation: From Neuroscience to Social Science*, Vol. 2: *Imitation, Human Development, and Culture*, Cambridge, MA: MIT Press, pp. 207–20.

Drinnan, A. and Lavender, T. (2006) "Deconstructing Delusions: A Qualitative Study Examining the Relationship between Religious Beliefs and Religious Delusions," *Mental Health, Religion & Culture* 9, no. 4: 317–31.

Durkheim, E. (1951) *Suicide: A Study in Sociology*, Glencoe, IL: The Free Press.

Eilan, N. (2001) "Meaning, Truth, and the Self: Commentary on Campbell, and Parnas and Sass," *Philosophy, Psychiatry & Psychology* 8, no. 2–3: 121–32.

Ellis, H. D. and Young, A. (1990) "Accounting for Delusional Misidentifications," *British Journal of Psychiatry* 157: 239–48.

Ellis, H. D., Young, A., Quale, A. and de Pauw, K. (1997) "Reduced Autonomic Responses to Faces in Capgras Delusion," *Proceedings of the Royal Society B: Biological Sciences* 264: 1085–92.

Eysenck, H. J. (1991) "Is Suggestibility?" in J. F. Schumaker (ed.) *Human Suggestibility: Advances in Theory, Research, and Application*. London: Routledge, pp. 76–83.

Felman, S. (1975) "Madness and Philosophy or Literature's Reason," *Yale French Studies* 52: 206–28.

Fine, C. (2006) *A Mind of Its Own: How Your Brain Distorts and Deceives*, New York: W. W. Norton & Co.

Fish, F. (1964) "The Cycloid Psychoses," *Comprehensive Psychiatry* 5: 155–69.

Foucault, M. (2006/1961) *History of Madness*, trans. J. Murphy and J. Khalfa, London and New York: Routledge.

Frankish, J. (2009) "Delusions: A Two-Level Framework," in M. Broome and L. Bortolotti (eds) *Psychiatry as Cognitive Neuroscience*. Oxford: Oxford University Press, pp. 269–84.

Freud, S. (1959/1922) *Group Psychology and the Analysis of the Ego*, trans. James Strachey, London: Hogarth Press.

Frith, C. D. (1992) *The Cognitive Neuropsychology of Schizophrenia*, Hove, UK: Psychology Press.

Frye, M. (1983) *The Politics of Reality*, Trumansburg, NY: Crossing Press.

Fulford, K. W. (1991) "Evaluative Delusions: Their Significance for

Philosophy and Psychiatry," *British Journal of Psychiatry* 159 (suppl. 14): 108–12.

Fulton, J. F. and Bailey, P. (1929) "Tumors in the Region of the Third Ventricle: Their Diagnosis and Relation to Pathological Sleep," *Journal of Nervous and Mental Disorders* 69: 1–25.

Gailey, J. A. (2009) " 'Starving Is the Most Fun a Girl Can Have': The Pro-Ana Subculture as Edgework," *Critical Criminology* 17: 93–108.

Gallese, V. (2002) "The Manifold Nature of Interpersonal Relations: The Quest for a Common Mechanism," *Philosophical Transactions of the Royal Society of London B: Biological Sciences*, 358: 517–28.

Garety, P. and Freeman, D. (1999) "Cognitive Approaches to Delusions: A Critical Review of Theories and Evidence," *British Journal of Clinical Psychology* 38: 113–54.

Garety, P. and Hemsley, D. (1994) *Delusions: Investigations into the Psychology of Delusional Reasoning*, Oxford: Oxford University Press.

Ghaemi, S. N. (2003) *The Concepts of Psychiatry: A Pluralistic Approach to Mind and Men*, Baltimore, MD: Johns Hopkins University Press.

—— (2004) "The Perils of Belief: Delusions Reexamined," *Philosophy, Psychiatry & Psychology* 11, no. 1: 49–54.

Gillet, G. (1994) "Insight, Delusion, and Belief," *Philosophy, Psychiatry & Psychology* 1, no. 4: 227–36.

Gilman, S. L. (1985) *Difference and Pathology*, Ithaca, NY: Cornell University Press.

Greenberg, D., Witzum, E. and Buchbinder, J. T. (1992) "Mysticism and Psychosis: The Fate of Ben Zoma," *British Journal of Medical Psychology* 65: 223–35.

Haizmann, C. (1982) *Diary*, in D. Peterson (ed.) *A Mad People's History of Madness*, Pittsburgh: University of Pittsburgh Press, p. 24.

Hambrook, C. (1996) "Obsessed," in J. Read and J. Reynolds (eds) *Speaking Our Minds: An Anthology*, London: Palgrave Macmillan, pp. 146–8.

Hamilton, A. (2007) "Against the Belief Model of Delusion," in M. Chung, W. Fulford and G. Graham (eds) *Reconceiving Schizophrenia*, Oxford: Oxford University Press, pp. 217–34.

Harré, R. and Tissaw, M. (2005) *Wittgenstein and Psychology: A Practical Guide*, Aldershot: Ashgate.

Hecker, J. F. C. (1846) *Epidemics of the Middle Ages*, trans. B. G. Babington, London: George Woodfall & Son.

Heidegger, M. (1962) *Being and Time*, trans. John Macquarrie and Edward Robinson. New York: Harper & Row.

Heinimaa, M. (2003) "Incomprehensibility," in B. Fulford, K. Morris, J. Sadler and G. Stanghellini (eds), *Nature and Narrative: An Introduction to the New Philosophy of Psychiatry*, Oxford: Oxford University Press, pp. 217–30.

Hesse-Biber, S. N. (2007) *The Cult of Thinness*, New York: Oxford University Press.

Hirstein, W. (2005) *Brain Fiction: Self-deception and the Riddle of Confabulation*, Cambridge, MA: MIT Press.

Hobbes, T. (1968/1651) *The Leviathan*, ed. C. B. Macpherson, London: Penguin.

Hsu, L. K. (1996) "Epidemiology of Eating Disorders," *Psychiatric Clinics of North America*, 19: 681–700.

Hunter, R. and Macalpine, I. (1982) *Three Hundred Years of Psychiatry 1535–1860: A History Presented in Selected English Texts*, Hartsdale, NY: Carlisle Publishing.

Hurlburt, R. T. (1990) *Sampling Normal and Schizophrenic Inner Experience*, New York: Plenum Press.

—— (1993) *Sampling Inner Experience in Disturbed Effect*, New York: Plenum Press.

Hurlburt, R. T. and Schwitzgebel, E. (2007) *Describing Inner Experience? Proponent Meets Skeptic*, Cambridge, MA: MIT Press.

Hurley, S. and Chater, N. (eds) (2005) *Perspectives on Imitation: From Neuroscience to Social Science*, vols 1 and 2, Cambridge, MA: MIT Press.

Jackson, M. C. (2007) "The Clinician's Illusion and Benign Psychosis," in M. C. Chung, W. Fulford and G. Graham (eds) *Reconceiving Schizophrenia*, Oxford: Oxford University Press, pp. 235–54.

Jackson, M. C. and Fulford, K. W. M. (1997) "Spiritual Experience and Psychopathology," *Philosophy, Psychiatry & Psychology* 4, no. 1: 41–65.

Jackson, S. (1986) *Melancholia and Depression: From Hippocratic Times to Modern Times*, New Haven, CT: Yale University Press.

James, W. (1961) *The Varieties of Religious Experience*, New York: Collier Books.

Jaspers, K. (1997/1913) *General Psychopathology*, 2 vols, ed. P. R. McHugh, Baltimore, MD: Johns Hopkins University Press.

Kant, I. (1978) *Anthropology from a Pragmatic Point of View*, trans. Victor L. Dowdell. Carbondale and Edwardsville, IL: Southern Illinois University Press.

Kaplan, B. (1964) *The Inner World of Mental Illness*, New York: Harper & Row.

Karimi, S., Windmann, S., Gunturkun, O. and Abraham, A. (2007) "Insight Problem Solving in Individuals with High versus Low Schizotypy," *Journal of Research in Personality* 41, no. 2: 473–80.

Kaysen, S. (1993) *Girl, Interrupted*, New York: Random House.

Kempf, L., Hussain, N. and Potash, J. B. (2005) "Mood Disorder with Psychotic Features, Schizoaffective Disorder, and Schizophrenia with Mood Features: Trouble at the Borders," *International Review of Psychiatry* 17: 9–19.

Kendler, K. S. and Gardner, C. O. (1998) "Boundaries of Major Depression: An Evaluation of DSM-IV Criteria," *American Journal of Psychiatry* 155, no. 2: 172–7.

Kim, C., Kim, J., Lee, M. and Kang, M. (2003) "Delusional Parasitosis as 'Folie à Deux'," *Journal of Korean Medical Science* 18: 462–5.

Kimhy, D., Goetz, R., Yale, S., Corcoran, C. and Malaspina, D. (2005) "Delusions in Individuals with Schizophrenia: Factor Structure, Clinical Correlates, and Putative Neurobiology," *Psychopathology* 38, no. 6: 338–44.

Kingdon, D. G. and Turkington, D. (1994) *Cognitive-Behavioural Therapy of Schizophrenia*, Hove, UK: Lawrence Erlbaum.

Kirmayer, L., Corin, E. and Jarvis, G. E. (2004) "Inside Knowledge: Cultural Constructions of Insight in Psychosis," in X. Amador and A. David (eds) *Insight and Psychosis: Awareness of Illness in Schizophrenia and Related Disorders*, 2nd edn, Oxford: Oxford University Press, pp. 197–230.

Kittay, E. (1987) *Metaphor: Its Cognitive Force and Linguistic Structure*, Oxford: Clarendon Press.

Klee, R. (2004) "Why Some Delusions Are Necessarily Inexplicable Beliefs," *Philosophy, Psychiatry & Psychology* 11, no. 1: 25–34.

Kraepelin, E. (1920) *Textbook of Psychiatry*, 8th edn, trans. R. Mary Barclay, ed. G. Robertson, Birmingham, AL: Classics of Medicine Library.

—— (1921) *Manic Depressive Insanity and Paranoia*, ed. R. M. Barclay, New York: Arno Press.

Kraus, A. (2007) "Schizophrenic Delusion and Hallucination as the Expression and Consequence of an Alteration of the Existential a Prioris," in M. C. Chung, B. Fulford and G. Graham (eds) *Reconceiving Schizophrenia*, Oxford: Oxford University Press, pp. 97–113.

Koenig, H. G. (2009) Research on Religion, Spirituality, and Mental Health: A Review," *Canadian Journal of Psychiatry* 54, no. 5: 283–91.

Lackey, J. and Sosa, E. (eds) (2006) *The Epistemology of Testimony*, Oxford: Clarendon Press.

Laing, R. D. (1959) *The Divided Self: An Existential Study in Sanity and Madness*, New York: Penguin Books.

Lakoff, G. and Johnson, M. (1980) *Metaphors We Live By*, Chicago: University of Chicago Press.

Langton, R. (1993) "Speech Acts and Unspeakable Acts," *Philosophy & Public Affairs*, 22, no. 4: 293–330.

Lazarus, A. (1986) "Folie à Deux in Identical Twins: Interaction of Nature and Nurture," *British Journal of Psychiatry* 148: 463–5.

Lazdgue, C. and Falret, J. (1877) "La Folie à deux ou folie communiqué," *Annals of Medical Psychology* 18: 321–55; repr. as "La Folie à deux (ou folie communiqué)," *American Journal of Psychiatry* 121 (suppl. 4) (1964): 1S–23S.

Leudar, I. and Thomas, P. (2001) *Voices of Reason, Voices of Insanity: Studies of Verbal Hallucinations*, London: Routledge.

Lifton, J. R. (1969) *Thought Reform and the Psychology of Totalism: A Study of "Brainwashing" in China*, New York: W. W. Norton & Co.

Livesley, W. J. (1998) "Suggestions for a Framework for an Empirically Based Classification of Personality Disorder," *Canadian Journal of Psychiatry* 43, no. 2 (March): 137–47.

MacDonald, N. (1960) "The Other Side: Living with Schizophrenia," *Canadian Medical Association Journal* 82: 218–21.

Mackay, C. (1993) *Extraordinary Popular Delusions and the Madness of Crowds*, New York: Barnes & Noble.

Maher, B. (1988) "Anomalous Experience and Delusional Thinking: The Logic of Explanations," in T. Oltmanns (ed.) *Delusional Beliefs*, Oxford: John Wiley & Sons, pp. 15–33.

Matossian, M. K. (1989) *Poisons of the Past: Molds, Epidemics, and History*, New Haven, CT: Yale University Press.

McKenna, P. J. (1984) "Disorders with Overvalued Ideas," *British Journal of Psychiatry* 145: 579–85.

McLaughlin, B. P. (2008) "Monothematic Delusions and Existential Feelings," in T. Bayne and J. Fernández (eds) *Delusion and Self-Deception: Affective and Motivational Influences on Belief Formation*, New York: Psychology Press, pp. 187–225.

Meltzoff, A. and Prinz, W. (eds) (2002) *The Imitative Mind: Development, Evolution, and Brain Bases*, Cambridge: Cambridge University Press.

Munro, A. (1999) *Delusional Disorder: Paranoia and Related Illnesses*, Cambridge: Cambridge University Press.

Murphy, D. (2006) *Psychiatry in the Scientific Image*, Cambridge, MA: MIT Press.

Musalek, M. (2003) "Meaning and Causes of Delusions," in B. Fulford, K. Morris, J. Sadler and G. Stanghellini (eds) *Nature and Narrative: An Introduction to the New Philosophy of Psychiatry*, Oxford: Oxford University Press, pp. 155–69.

Nasar, S. (1998) *A Beautiful Mind*, New York: Touchstone.

Ng, F. (2007) "The Interface between Religion and Psychosis," *Australasian Psychiatry* 15, no. 1: 62–6.

Nijinsky, V. (1995) *The Diary of Vaslav Nijinsky*, ed. J. Acocella, New York: Farrar, Straus & Giroux.

Oltmanns, T. F. (1988) *Delusional Beliefs*, Oxford: John Wiley & Sons.

Pargament, K. I. (1997) *The Psychology of Religion and Coping*, New York: Guildford Press.

Persinger, M. A. and Healey, F. (2002) "Experimental Facilitation of the Sensed Presence: Possible Intercalation between the Hemispheres Induced by Complex Magnetic Fields," *Journal of Nervous and Mental Disorders* 190: 533–41.

Peters, E., Day, S., McKenna, J. and Orbach, G. (1999) "Delusional Ideation in Religious and Psychotic Populations," *British Journal of Clinical Psychology* 38, no. 1: 83–96.

Peterson, D. (ed.) (1984) *A Mad People's History of Madness*, Pittsburgh, PA: University of Pittsburgh Press.

Phillips, J. (1996) "Key Concepts: Hermeneutics," *Philosophy, Psychiatry & Psychology* 3: 61–9.

Phillips, K. A., Kim, J. M. and Hudson, J. (1995) "Body Image Disturbance in Body Dysmorphic Disorder and Eating Disorders: Obsessions or Delusions?" *Psychiatric Clinics of North America* 18, no. 20: 317–34.

Pillay, S., Bodkin, J. A. and Shapiro, E. (1998) "Psychotic Acts: The Question of Meaning," *Harvard Review of Psychiatry* 6: 38–43.

Pitkin, H. (2009) "Mental Illness is Indeed a Myth," in M. Broome and L. Bortolotti (eds) *Psychiatry as Cognitive Neuroscience: Philosophical Perspectives*, Oxford: Oxford University Press, pp. 83–101.

Pope, A. (1711) *An Essay on Criticism*, London: Lewis.

Potter, N. N. (2000) "Giving Uptake," *Social Theory and Practice* 26, no. 3: 479–508.

Puri, B. K., Lekh, S., Nijran, K. S., Bagary, M. S. and Richardson, A. J. (2001) "SPECT Neuroimaging in Schizophrenia with Religious Delusions," *International Journal of Psychophysiology* 40: 143–8.

Radden, J. (2007) "Defining Persecutory Paranoia," in M. C. Chung, B. Fulford and G. Graham (eds) *Reconceiving Schizophrenia*, Oxford: Oxford University Press, pp. 255–73.

—— (2008) "My Symptoms, Myself: Reading Mental Illness Memoirs for Identity Assumptions," in H. Clarke (ed.) *Depression and Narrative: Telling the Dark*, New York: SUNY Press, pp. 15–28.

—— (Forthcoming) "Insightlessness, the Deflationary Turn, " *Philosophy, Psychiatry & Psychology*.

Reimer, M. (Forthcoming) "Treatment Adherence in the Absence of Insight: A Puzzle and a Proposed Solution," *Philosophy, Psychiatry & Psychology*.

Reznek, L. *Delusion and the Madness of the Masses*, Rowman & Littlefield Publishing Inc. (in press).

Rhodes, J. and Gipps, R. (2008) "Delusions, Certainty, and the Background," *Philosophy, Psychiatry & Psychology* 15, no. 4: 295–310.

Rhodes, J. and Jakes, S. (2004) "The Contribution of Metaphor and Metonymy to Delusions," *Psychology and Psychotherapy: Theory, Research and Practice* 77: 1–17.

Roberts, G. (1999) "The Rehabilitation of Rehabilitation: A Narrative Approach to Psychosis," in G. Roberts and J. Holmes (eds) *Healing Stories: Narrative in Psychiatry and Psychotherapy*, Oxford: Oxford University Press, pp. 152–80.

Sacks, H. M., Carpenter, W. T. and Strauss, J. (1974) "Recovery from Delusions: Three Phases Documented by Patient's Interpretation of Research," *Archives of General Psychiatry* 30, no. 1 (January): 117–20.

Sacks, O. (1984) *A Leg to Stand On*, New York: Harper & Row.

Sadler, J. Z. (2005) *Values and Psychiatric Diagnosis*, Oxford: Oxford University Press.

Samuels, R. (2009) "Delusions as a Natural Kind," in M. Broome and L. Bortolotti (eds) *Psychiatry as Cognitive Neuroscience: Philosophical Perspectives*, Oxford: Oxford University Press, pp. 49–82.

Sargant, W. (1957) *Battle for the Mind: A Physiology of Conversion and Brain-washing.* New York: Doubleday & Co.

Sartre, J.-P. (1956) *Being and Nothingness,* trans. Hazel Barnes, New York: Citadel Press.

Sass, L. (1994) *The Paradoxes of Delusion,* Ithaca, NY: Cornell University Press.

Sass, L. and Parnass, J. (2001) "Phenomenology of Self-Disturbances in Schizophrenia: Some Research Findings and Directions," *Philosophy, Psychiatry & Psychology* 8, no. 4: 347–56.

Saver, J. and Rabin, J. (1997) "The Neural Substrates of Religious Experience," *Journal of Neuropsychiatry and Clinical Neuroscience* 9: 498–510.

Schneider, K. (1959) *Clinical Psychopathy,* ed. M. W. Hamilton, Oxford: Grune & Stratton.

Schopenhauer, A. (1995/1818) *The World as Will and Idea,* trans. Jill Berman, London: J. M. Dent.

Schreber, D. (2000) *Memoirs of My Nervous Illness,* trans. Ida Macalpine and Richard A. Hunter, New York: New York Review of Books Classics.

Schumaker, J. F. (ed.) (1991) *Human Suggestibility: Advances in Theory, Research, and Application,* London: Routledge.

Sechehaye, M. (1994) *Autobiography of a Schizophrenic Girl: The True Story of "Renee,"* trans. Grace Rubin-Rabson, New York: Meridian.

Shimizu, M., Kubota, Y., Toichi, M. and Baba, H. (2007) "Folie à deux and Shared Psychotic Disorder," *Current Psychiatry Reports* 9: 200–5.

Shimmel, S. (1992) *The Seven Deadly Sins,* New York: Oxford University Press.

Shiwach, R. S. and Sobin, P. B. (1998) "Monozygotic Twins, Folie à Deux and Heritability: A Case Report and Critical Review," *Medical Hypotheses* 50: 369–74.

Siddle, R., Haddock, G., Tarrier, N. and Faragher, E. B. (2004) "Religious Beliefs and Religious Delusions: Response to Treatment in Schizophrenia," *Mental Health, Religion & Culture* 7, no. 3: 211–23.

Sims, A. C. P. (1992) "Symptoms and Beliefs," *Journal of the Royal Society of Health* 122: 42–6.

—— (2003) *Symptoms in the Mind: An Introduction to Descriptive Psychopathology,* London: Saunders.

Smith, D. (2007) *Muses, Madmen, and Prophets: Rethinking the History, Science, and Meaning of Auditory Hallucinations,* New York: Penguin Books.

Soskice, J. M. (1985) *Metaphor and Religious Language*, Oxford: Clarendon Press.

Spitzer, M. (1990) "On Defining Delusions," *Comprehensive Psychiatry* 31, no. 5: 377–97.

Stanghellini, G. (2007) "Schizophrenia and the Sixth Sense," in M. C. Chung, B. Fulford and G. Graham (eds) *Reconceiving Schizophrenia*, Oxford: Oxford University Press, pp. 129–50.

Stephens, G. L. and Graham, G. (2007) "The Delusional Stance," in M. C. Chung, B. Fulford and G. Graham (eds) *Reconceiving Schizophrenia*, Oxford: Oxford University Press, pp. 193–215.

Stewart, D. (1854) *The Collected Works*, ed. W. Hamilton, Edinburgh: Thomas Constable & Co.

Stiver, D. (1996) *The Philosophy of Religious Language: Sign, Symbol, and Story*, New York: Blackwell.

Storr, A. (1997) *Feet of Clay: Saints, Sinners, and Madmen: A Study of Gurus*, New York: Simon & Schuster.

Thiher, A. (2002) *Revels in Madness: Insanity in Medicine and Literature*, Ann Arbor, MI: University of Michigan Press.

Thornton, T. (2007) *Essential Philosophy of Psychiatry*, Oxford: Oxford University Press.

Tirrell, L. (1993) "Definition and Power: Toward Authority without Privilege," *Hypatia* 8, no. 4: 1–34.

Torpor, A. (2001) *Managing the Contradictions: Recovery from Severe Mental Disorder*. Stockholm: Stockholm University Press.

Tsuang, M. T., Taylor, L. and Faraone, S. V. (2007) "An Overview of the Genetics of Psychotic Mood States," *Journal of Psychiatric Research* 38: 3–15.

Veale, D. (2002) "Over-valued Ideas: A Conceptual Analysis," *Behaviour Research and Therapy* 40, no. 4: 383–400.

Von Domarus, E. (1944) "The Specific Laws of Logic in Schizophrenia," L. Kasanin (ed.) *Language and Thought in Schizophrenia*, Berkeley, CA: University of California Press.

Wehmeier, P., Barth, N. and Remschmidt, H. (2003) "Induced Delusional Disorder: A Review of the Concept and an Unusual Case of Folie à Famille," *Psychopathology* 36, no. 1: 37–45.

Wernicke, C. (1900) "Outline of Psychiatry in Clinical Lectures," *Alienist and Neurologist* 20, no. 2: 267–316.

White, T. G. (1995) "Folie Simultanée in Monozygotic Twins," *Canadian Journal of Psychiatry* 40: 418–20.

Wittgenstein, L. (1969) *On Certainty*, trans. Denis Paul and G. E. M. Anscombe, New York: Harper & Row.

Zachar, P. (2000) "Psychiatric Disorders Are Not Natural Kinds," *Philosophy, Psychiatry & Psychology* 7: 167–82.

Zentner, M. (2002) "Arthur Schopenhauer (1788–1860)," in E. Erwin (ed.) *The Freud Encyclopedia: Theory, Therapy, and Culture*, New York: Routledge, pp. 371–4.

Index

Related titles from Routledge

On Courage – 'Thinking in Action'
Geoffrey Scarre

'Courage is a cardinal virtue and at the core of our everyday, lived morality. It raises some fascinating questions – can a criminal be courageous? Is the courageous person not afraid? – and yet contemporary philosophers have said surprisingly little about it. So this insightful, open-minded and accessible study will be especially valuable to anyone interested in the morality of the virtues.' – *Roger Crisp, St. Anne's College, Oxford, UK*

What is courage and why is it one of the oldest and most universally admired virtues? How is it relevant in the world today, and what contemporary forms does it take?

In this insightful and crisply written book, Geoffrey Scarre examines these questions and many more. He begins by defining courage, asking how it differs from fearlessness, recklessness and fortitude, and why people are often more willing to ascribe it to others than to avow it for themselves. He also asks whether courage can serve bad ends as well as good, and whether it can sometimes promote confrontation over compromise and dialogue.

On Courage explores the ideas of Aristotle, Aquinas and many later philosophers who have written about courage, as well as drawing on classic and recent examples of courage in politics and fiction, including the German anti-Nazi 'White Rose Movement', the modern phenomenon of 'whistle-blowing', and Stephen Crane's *The Red Badge of Courage*.

ISBN13: 978–0–415–47106–0 (Hbk)
ISBN13: 978–0–415–47113–8 (Pbk)
ISBN13: 978–0–203–85198–2 (Ebk)

Available at all good bookshops
For ordering and further information please visit:
www.routledge.com

Related titles from Routledge

Embodied Cognition –
'New Problems of Philosophy'
Lawrence Shapiro

'Embodied cognition is sweeping the planet and Larry Shapiro has just written the first comprehensive treatment of this exciting and new research program. This book is now, and for years to come will be, unquestionably the best way for students and researchers alike, to gain access to and learn to evaluate this exciting new research paradigm in cognitive science.' – *Fred Adams, University of Delaware, USA*

'*Embodied Cognition* is the first of its kind – a beautifully lucid and even-handed introduction to the many questions and issues that define the field of embodied cognition. Psychologists, neuroscientists, computer scientists, and philosophers should jump on this book. It promises to set the terms of debate in this exciting new enterprise for years to come.' – *Elliott Sober, University of Wisconsin Madison, USA*

Embodied cognition often challenges standard cognitive science. In this outstanding introduction Lawrence Shapiro sets out the central themes and debates surrounding embodied cognition, explaining and assessing the work of many of the key figures in the field, including Jerry Fodor, Hilary Putnam, Andy Clark and John Haugeland.

Beginning with an outline of the theoretical and methodological commitments of standard cognitive science, Shapiro then examines philosophical arguments surrounding the traditional perspective. He introduces topics such as dynamic systems theory, vision, attention, memory, and language, before addressing core issues in philosophy of mind such as personal identity and reductionism.

Including helpful chapter summaries and annotated further reading at the end of each chapter, *Embodied Cognition* is essential reading for all students of philosophy of mind and psychology, and cognitive science.

ISBN 13: 978–0–415–77341–6 (Hbk)
ISBN 13: 978–0–415–77342–3 (Pbk)
ISBN 13: 978–0–203–85066–4 (Ebk)

Available at all good bookshops
For ordering and further information please visit:

www.routledge.com

Related titles from Routledge

Self-Knowledge – 'New Problems of Philosophy'
Brie Gertler

How do you know your own thoughts and feelings? Do we have 'privileged access' to our own minds? Does introspection provide a grasp of a thinking self or 'I'?

The problem of self-knowledge is one of the most fascinating in all of philosophy and has crucial significance for the philosophy of mind and epistemology. In this outstanding introduction Brie Gertler assesses the leading theoretical approaches to self-knowledge, explaining the work of many of the key figures in the field: from Descartes and Kant, through to Bertrand Russell and Gareth Evans, as well as recent work by Tyler Burge, David Chalmers, William Lycan and Sydney Shoemaker.

Beginning with an outline of the distinction between self-knowledge and self-awareness and providing essential historical background to the problem, Gertler addresses specific theories of self-knowledge such as the acquaintance theory, the inner-sense theory, and the rationalist theory, as well as leading accounts of self-awareness. The book concludes with a critical explication of the dispute between empiricist and rationalist approaches.

Including helpful chapter summaries, annotated further reading and a glossary, *Self-Knowledge* is essential reading for students of philosophy of mind, epistemology, and metaphysics.

ISBN 13: 978–0–415–40525–6 (Hbk)
ISBN 13: 978–0–415–40526–3 (Pbk)
ISBN 13: 978–0–20–383567–8 (Ebk)

Available at all good bookshops
For ordering and further information please visit:
www.routledge.com

Related titles from Routledge

Arguing About the Mind

Edited by Brie Gertler and Lawrence Shapiro

'Arguing About the Mind makes use of original sources to introduce problems in the philosophy of mind in a way calculated to be intelligible to readers with no previous background in philosophy. By relying on readings intended for a broad audience, Gertler and Shapiro deftly sidestep technical disputes of the kind that too often deter students encountering serious philosophical writing for the first time. The result is a stunning topical introduction to philosophy via the philosophy of mind.' – *John Heil, Washington University in St Louis, USA*

'I think this is brilliant. In conception and execution, the anthology does something which is both original and needed as a teaching resource. Instead of taking tired old routes, the editors motivate the philosophical questions in a fresh and illuminating way, with an excellent choice of readings based around problems which will have occurred to most thoughtful philosophy students.' – *Tim Crane, University College London, UK*

Arguing About the Mind is a highly accessible, engaging introduction to the core questions in the philosophy of mind. This fresh, bold and exciting collection offers a selection of thought-provoking articles that examine a broad range of issues from the mind/body relation to animal and artificial intelligence.

The editors assemble some of the most influential and controversial contributions of key philosophers in the field including David Chalmers, Thomas Nagel, Daniel Dennett and Alan Turing, and challenge the reader to reflect on debates on:

- the problem of consciousness
- the nature of the mind
- the relationship between the mind, body and world
- the notion of selfhood
- pathologies and behavioural problems
- animal, machine and extra-terrestrial intelligence

The articles chosen are clear, interesting and free from unnecessary jargon. The editors provide lucid introductions to each section in which they give an overview of the debate and outline the arguments of the papers. *Arguing About the Mind* is an original and stimulating reader for students new to the philosophy of mind.

ISBN 10: 0–415–77162–5 (hbk)
ISBN 10: 0–415–77163–3 (pbk)
ISBN 13: 978–0–415–77162–7 (hbk)
ISBN 13: 978–0–415–77163–4 (pbk)

Available at all good bookshops
For ordering and further information please visit:

www.routledge.com